SO-AZM-801

Praise for

Tiny Homes

Anyone who wants to live small — but
comfortably — on our delicate planet
should snap up this fantastic guide.
Packed with persuasive in-depth
case studies, tips, and practical floor plans,
the book begs the question, "Do you really
need all that space?" Tiny homes are a unique,
21st-century way for us all to live within our
means, and in modest but unique fashion.

— Rebecca Martin, Group Editor,
Mother Earth News and *Grit*

To call *A Tiny Home to Call Your Own*
the bible of tiny house living would not be
an overstatement. In a well thought out and
organized manner, this book covers everything
that one should think about when deciding
whether or not to live in a tiny house and how
to go about doing it. For most people the idea of
"going tiny" is overwhelming and daunting.
I believe this book could be one of
the most potent tools to help someone
overcome the challenges to achieve their tiny
house dreams. I only wish that I had this
book when I built my tiny house!

— Rob Greenfield, author,
Dude Making a Difference

Pat has written an engaging and informative
guide for those who wish to consider living
lighter on the land and lighter on their budgets,
with step by step instructions and documented
case studies. We are challenged to examine our
own values as part of the design process.
Our perfect home may not resemble
the one constructed in our mind by
our preconceived notions.
This book clearly demonstrates that
we can indeed live large on a small footprint.

Whether the right size house for you is a tiny
house or something larger, this book will guide
you through the critical steps to create a dwelling
that is exactly what you need ... nothing more,
nothing less ... a perfect home.

— Heidi Louisa Schweizer,
architect & general contractor,
LEED AP – BD&C

A Tiny Home
to Call Your Own

SECOND EDITION 2

LIVING WELL IN
JUST-RIGHT HOUSES

PATRICIA FOREMAN

new society
PUBLISHERS

Copyright © 2019 by Patricia L. Foreman
All rights reserved.

Cover design by Diane McIntosh.
Cover image: ©iStock 477249808.
Woodgrain background: © Adobestock 72383843
Printed in Canada. First printing February 2019.

This book is intended to be educational and informative. It is not intended to serve as a guide. The author and publisher disclaim all responsibility for any liability, loss, or risk that may be associated with the application of any of the contents of this book.

Inquiries regarding requests to reprint all or part of *A Tiny Home to Call Your Own* should be addressed to New Society Publishers at the address below. To order directly from the publishers, please call toll-free (North America 1-800-567-6772), or order online at www.newsociety.com.

Any other inquiries can be directed by mail to

New Society Publishers
P.O. Box 189, Gabriola Island, BC V0R 1X0, Canada
250-247-9737

LIBRARY AND ARCHIVES CANADA CATALOGUING IN PUBLICATION

Title: A tiny home to call your own : living well in just-right houses / Patricia Foreman.

Names: Foreman, Patricia L. (Patricia Louise), 1950- author.

Description: Second edition. | Includes bibliographical references and index.

Identifiers: Canadiana (print) 20190053011 | Canadiana (ebook) 20190053062 | ISBN 9780865718906 (softcover) | ISBN 9781550926835 (PDF) | ISBN 9781771422796 (EPUB)

Subjects: LCSH: Small houses. | LCSH: Architecture, Domestic.

Classification: LCC NA7533 .F67 2019 | DDC 728/.37—dc23

Funded by the Government of Canada

Financé par le gouvernement du Canada

Canada

New Society Publishers' mission is to publish books that contribute in fundamental ways to building an ecologically sustainable and just society, and to do so with the least possible impact on the environment, in a manner that models this vision.

FSC
www.fsc.org
MIX
Paper from responsible sources
FSC® C016245

Certified
B Corporation

new society
PUBLISHERS

*Dedicated to all home dwellers
who are enjoying a larger life in well-fitting homes.*

Contents

Introduction

W HY A BOOK ABOUT TINY HOMES? Because when you really look at the U.S. housing inventory, you see that Americans have become obsessed with BIG. From supersized to jumbo. This includes soft drinks, vehicles, and housing. Not everyone wants, needs, or can afford the American Dream JUMBO home.

R. Buckminster Fuller advised his students to look for the "gaps" in any field. Find the gaps and develop a profitable way to fill them and you will never be lacking for a job or meaningful, useful work to do. In looking at housing many people realize there is a huge gap in choices between what is available and what they want.

Homeowners and house renters in our society can choose from two basic options: (1) huge, mini-mansions that are larger than they really need on the upscale or (2) cheaply made starter homes and plastic single-wide and double-wide manufactured homes on the lower end.

The 2010 Census enumerated that the 309 million people in the U.S. lived in 117 million households. That's an average of 2.6 people per household.[1] What is even more dramatic is that

Very little is currently available in U.S. housing that is small yet high quality, handcrafted, and built with individual class and personality. Tiny homes help fill that gap.

1

between 1999 and 2014, the number of single-person households went up to about 34.2 million (from 26.6 million).[2] That translates to more than ten percent of the U.S. population living alone in 2014.

The trend is clear. Single-person households are expected to reach around 41 million by 2030, an average annual rise of 1.1 percent over 2015–2030."[3] Single-person households don't need, or even want, a biggie McMansion.

The takeaway is that the average American dream house of three bedrooms, two baths, and a two-car garage is rapidly becoming outdated.

With baby boomers approaching retirement, and more professional single folks in the marketplace, the demand for quality, smaller custom housing is destined to skyrocket. It's a trend that needs to happen on every level: sociologically, environmentally, and economically. People are asking themselves: "How much is enough?"

While it is true that homebuilders can build any size home you want, most contractors have told us over and over, "There isn't any profit in building small houses. The big bucks are made with big houses." This is only partly true.

HomeAdvisor states that "the average cost to build a new house in America comes in at $288,642, which would put a 2,000-square-foot home costing about $150 per square foot. This will obviously vary greatly with all the cost variables involved, so the cost could range between $151,839 and $425,445".[4]

As a really rough example, you might expect that if a 2,000-square-foot house at $150 per square foot costs $289,000 to build, then a 1,000-square-foot tiny house would cost $145,500.

It isn't that simple. Smaller homes often cost more per square foot to build. This is because smaller houses have the features of a larger house (kitchen and bathrooms) that are much more costly per square foot to build compared with other rooms in a house, such as bedrooms, sunrooms, and "bonus" rooms.

That is why tiny and smaller houses can be more expensive per square foot but less expensive overall.

Now here's a big money question. Big houses cost more than little homes. But are they better investments? An article in the May 20, 2001, *Seattle Times*, written by Elizabeth Rhodes, states,

> Judged not on sales price, but on the cost per square foot — which reveals how much buyers actually get for their money — little houses outperform their bigger brethren not by a little, but by a lot. In the past decade, homes 2,500 square feet or larger have appreciated 57 percent. In 2000 that put the square-foot price at $147. But those under 1,200 square feet — in other words your basic two-bedroom, one-bath starter house — have appreciated a remarkable 78 percent to $184 per square foot in 2000.[5]

Small homes appreciated more per square foot than larger houses. Why? Because overall, the smaller houses were more affordable and therefore had more demand from a larger buyer base. That small-home buyer base is rapidly expanding.

Many people are attracted to tiny homes, cabins, cottages, and bungalows not only because they are more affordable but also because they can be so functional and personal. We define tiny homes as any full-featured, smaller house from about 350 square feet up to about 1,000 square feet, and even as large as 1,500 square feet.

The square footage definition we are using for a tiny home is relative. Sarah Susanka defines a "not so big house" as being from 2,000 to 3,000 square feet. It is all relative to one's needs and idea of a small or large space.

Now, we can't snap a chalk line and say 1,100 square feet is *not* a tiny home — size truly varies depending on individual perspectives. Let's not get stuck on the square footage of "my small house is smaller than your small house."

Here's the bottom line: you can live in an attractive, aesthetically appealing upscale tiny/small house *and* do it so that your home is quality built, architecturally beautiful, personally delightful, highly marketable, and profitable.

The basis of this book is that small in housing can be beautiful, functional, and economical and ecological.

Another problem we find in defining what is correctly sized housing is that our language doesn't have the vocabulary to adequately describe the features and benefits of living in tiny homes.

Tiny home adjectives seem to be limited to "cozy" and "cute." But tiny homes offer so much more than cute. They can be magical. Well-built tiny homes have the warm, fuzzy feeling of home at their primal core. They can offer personal safety and deep contentment.

Living in tiny homes can be truly magical because once inside them you naturally set your perception levels differently. You notice smaller things. Your intuition and senses pick up changes more easily, especially in subtle energies. The faintest smells are more noticeable. There is a totally different ambiance in, and around, a tiny home than there is in a big house. When you go into a large home you are *inside*. The inside air, temperature, ambiance is different. When you are in a tiny home, the outside seems closer. The air is different. Feelings can be differently perceived.

For example, you get a feeling of being closer to nature. Not as close as camping in a tent but certainly closer than in a full-size house. The things I find most enjoyable are hearing birds' songs at daybreak, the wind blowing and rustling the leaves, rain on the roof, and the sound of snowfall. The elements are more intimate to my personal environment. It is like being in a small boat on the ocean. The waxing and waning of energy currents of water or air help one feel the rhythms of life and the heartbeat of nature.

Having a very compact kitchen makes it efficient to cook and prepare meals. You don't have to take many steps to do any task. Often you just turn around. For example, an eat-in kitchen is much easier and more efficient to care for than a dining room separate from the kitchen.

Imagine that your entire house can be vacuumed with the cord plugged into one central outlet. A few minutes each day is more than enough to sweep the house. You might even leave the vacuum plugged in, sitting, waiting for action.

There is also a feeling of confidence and clarity I have when not surrounded by too many things. It is Zen-like. When there are too many things, I get a closed-in claustrophobic feeling even in the largest of rooms. Tiny homes have a way of forcing one to focus on clutter and disorganization. Living in mine enabled me to reorder my life so that I kept the few things that are most important to me versus the many things that cluttered my space and my mind.

I spend less time looking for things. It's estimated that the average person spends at least 30 minutes each day looking for things. That's an average of 14 hours per month of frustrated searching. Keeping clutter under control can be a major resource for finding spare time. Chapter Seven on "stuffology" goes into the cost of clutter in detail.[6]

Living in small places forces you to focus on what is important in life and what isn't. This includes time for friends, studying topics that interest you, or even community service — wherever your sacred soul contract might lead. Let's face it, larger homes can be distracting by the sheer volume of things that need to be done and maintained. So much so that you can be held back from doing and being what is really important in your life.

So, how do you make a tiny house a home? You do it through architectural detail, very efficient use of space, and the personal touches that put art and craftsmanship back into the building of a home. You minimize transitional spaces like hallways and stairwells and increase transition zones to the outdoors. You maximize the use of storage areas with organization and vertical storage. You create an environment that is not just expensive heated storage for stuff but an environment that supports you, your interests, and your lifestyle. You make a house that's your home and enables your life-style(s).

Recipe for a Tiny Home

What to Add and What to Leave Out

What makes tiny seem small and big appear huge — supersize from already-jumbo? How much is enough? Here are a few considerations, tips and tricks.

What to Add to a Tiny Home	What to Leave Out of a Tiny Home
Add creative, well-planned rooms and home designs.	Omit more heated space than you really need.
Use a well-thought-out floor plan that minimizes hallways, stairwells, and other dead spaces that aren't routinely or functionally used.	Leave out large hallways, stairs, closets that occupy square footage space that you have to heat, clean, and pay for.
Add universal design features that simplify life by making the home usable by more people at different stages of their lives and do so with little or no extra cost.	Leave out home features that make accessibility and usability difficult for some folks. This includes steep steps, hard-to-open doors with round knobs, high shelves.
Add details and personal touches that bring a home alive with your personality and nurture your spirit.	Leave out the molded plastic look that is artificial, boring, and common.

What to Add to a Tiny Home	What to Leave Out of a Tiny Home
Add easy-care landscaping that doesn't require you to mow so much in your spare time. Add gardens for beauty and self-reliant food production.	Leave out lots of grass and high-maintenance plants that demand your time for mowing, weeding, mulching, and trimming.
Be able to vacuum each level so your sweeper can reach every corner from the same electrical outlet. This is a genuine cleaning timesaver.	Leave out multiple levels and rooms that have hard-to-get-into corners that are difficult to reach.
Bring the outdoors in with well-placed and right-sized windows that allow natural light and maximize views for a sense of geomancy. Design connecting views from room to room to give a sense of spaciousness.	Don't use a floor plan that doesn't consider a home's views, natural day lighting, and solar gain or loss.
Add decks and porches to inexpensively expand unheated floor space and provide a transition from the yard or street into the home. Provide relaxing places to chat, sip tea, or host a party.	Many conventional houses don't offer porches or patios where it is comfortable to sit and visit. This guarantees you will spend 100 percent of your time indoors and have little contact with the world outside your front door.
Create rooms that you can use for more than one purpose. In permaculture, multifunctionality is called "stacking."	Leave out rarely used spaces and formal areas that function only occasionally for holidays, parties, or storage.
Add lots of built-in storage: book shelves, under-bed drawers, or space saver closets. Keep only those things that serve and please you; dispose of the rest. Design spaces that help minimize clutter.	Do not have closet space without shelves or space organizers. Omit rooms that give you very little feeling for home or coziness. Incorporate curves instead of having only square angles.

What to Add to a Tiny Home	What to Leave Out of a Tiny Home
Use space that is thoughtfully designed in detail, compact without being cramped.	Leave out ostentatious square footage and sprawling space.
Include different ceiling heights to give variety and take away any boxy feeling.	Leave out ceilings that are so high they have an impersonal feeling and literally leave you feeling cold because the warmer air rises to the ceiling away from your body.
Use fun colors both inside and out.	Gray, off-white, vanilla, tend to be boring colors.
Go for quality over quantity in every detail, thing, and use.	Leave out stuff you buy because the price is cheap not because you need it. Omit redundancy.

Chapter 1

Is a Tiny Home Right for You?

A S TINY HOUSE BUILDERS, whenever we are talking with someone we've just met and the concept of tiny homes comes up, people usually react with, "What a great idea!" Then as we explain the many uses for tiny homes, inevitably the conversation gets around to how they could use one, or they know of someone who could. We have yet to have any negative, nay-sayer responses to the tiny homes concept.

Folks make inquiries about tiny homes from all age groups and socioeconomic classes. There is a growing sector of people wanting less of a mortgage and more of a life, both of which are inherently possible with tiny homes.

Tiny home lovers are those like ourselves who want to live in less space. Not necessarily because we can't afford more but because of the advantages smaller homes offer. We have a broad range of interests that are more fulfilling to us than cleaning, harboring possessions (clutter), and paying excessive real estate and personal property taxes.

More and more of us are making our lifestyles a statement of our political, spiritual, and environmental beliefs. Few of us need excessive stuff as a substitute for self-esteem. We even know millionaires who live in tiny homes or want smaller homes so they can be free to pursue their soul's passion and service.

Below we identify a few of the kinds of people interested in tiny homes and the many uses for tiny homes.

People Who Might be Interested in Tiny Homes
Downsizers

This group is huge and includes almost everyone seeking a simpler life. Downsizers are folks shedding and discarding things and stuff that either no longer serve them or for which they no longer have any high regard. They are cleaning out closets and sorting through items in basements, attics, and garages. They are recycling their unused and unwanted possessions through charities such as Goodwill, Habitat for Humanity, church and hospital consignment shops or through yard sales, moving sales, the classifieds, and dumpsters.

If you prefer to give your unwanted items directly to people who can use them then, try freecycle.org, a website established specifically to help people help each other directly.

I have periodically downsized with the conscious intent of tithing and recycling. When I cull books from my many bookshelves, I donate them to people or institutions who are able to use them, including libraries, prisons, and individuals. I call this "book tithing."

In ancient times, tithing referred to leaving part of the harvest to go back into and replenish the soil. It also referred to saving ten percent of the seeds for next year's planting. Today, tithing means giving money or in-kind contributions to charitable purposes.

There are many forms of tithing, including clothes tithing, tool tithing, and furniture and art tithing. Adding the concept of tithing to giveaways lends a service component and intrinsic value to an item because someone else can use it. This takes more effort and conscious intent than just dumping stuff in the dumpster and filling up our landfills. It is far more rewarding to help others and honor the value of an item that is still usable.

Recently, I helped a dear friend clear and separate her stuff from a ten-year marriage. The marriage differences were irreconcilable and divorce the only viable option. As we were taking things to the dumpster and sorting through her many beautiful things, she said many times, "Is this what it was all about?" She was referring to all the things. Were things more the center of focus than the marriage itself? Was their marriage so wrapped up in stuffology that they forgot the importance of honoring and serving each other?

Downsizers are those who are decreasing the amount of stuff in their lives. This includes folks whose life patterns have changed, possibly through unemployment, retirement, death, illness, separation, or divorce. Some are re-treading for a different career, to get more education, or to follow new life patterns and directions. Shedding old stuff and old ways often opens the door for a new and expanded life to begin.

Empty Nesters

Kids grow up and leave. That's what they are supposed to do, right? That means more bedrooms and baths than the parents need. As life changes, so do housing needs.

Boomerangs and Nest Returners

Do you have that special child who won't, or can't, leave the nest — or keeps coming back, and back, and back home? Are all your kids nicknamed "boomerang"? Life situations change; sometimes family members need a place to land. Having a separate place for them to land (like a detached tiny home in the backyard) might make your life easier.

Preretirement and Retirees

You've worked hard all your life and now it's time to step down. You may be taking some well deserved time off or changing careers or moving to a new location. The best part is yet to come. With the educational opportunities and web-based training that are available, many people are having multiple careers. One of my personal mottoes is "retire early and often." Life is too precious to spend in a job or career you are not passionate about. And, let's face it — once you have done something for an extended period of time you may grow tired of it, in which case it might be time to learn and do something new. Go for everything in life you want — at any age.

The Sandwich Generation

There is a large need for housing for those who are still caring for their children and suddenly have to also start caring for aging parents. This is the sandwich generation. Over 20 percent of us baby boomers (born between 1946 and 1964) could be in the position of having our parents and our children or grandchildren living with us. These multigenerational families in need of more and varied living spaces are perfect candidates for one (or more) tiny homes in the backyard — or back 40 acres.

Semi-Assisted-Living Individuals

There are times in our lives when we all need help. This may be in the form of assisted living that we might need at any age. This could include after having surgery or not being able to fully function during a recovery period, whether it's physical, mental, financial, or any disruptive situation setbacks that life brings forth. Sometimes a place of refuge helps one get through.

Semi-assisted living might also involve a situation where a parent or someone we know is simply not ready for a retirement community. They are able to take care of themselves and want their independence. However, it would be convenient and bring a lot of peace of mind to have them close by. A tiny home close by might make all the difference.

Most assisted-living facilities today cost an average of $3,000 to $5,000 per month. At this rate it doesn't take many months before you could own a tiny house free and clear and still have some inheritance in the wings.

Parents, Grandparents, and Extended Family

Tiny homes might be especially valuable for a parent, family member, or dear friend who wants to live close by or have a place to stay when they visit for extended periods of time.

This doesn't mean this person is poor or lacking in finances because they might live in a tiny home. They might be quite well off, but money isn't everything. Close relationships are worth much more than money. To have a grandparent helping to raise your children might bring a wisdom, family history, and trans-generational bond that literally extends your family.

Many people, especially older folks, sometimes feel useless. They feel they don't have anything to get up for in the mornings. Their life is lonely and empty. Mother Theresa said it well: "One of the greatest diseases is to be nobody to anybody."

Socrates famous saying "The unexamined life is not worth living" might also be stated as "A life without a purpose is a life not worth living." Perhaps tiny homes can help give purpose and meaning to lives that are otherwise empty.

A tiny home can often be put on an existing lot as a granny unit, without having to purchase a separate lot — check with your local zoning board. This is called a granny flat in California. In Canada this is often called a secondary suite.

Single Professionals

There is a trend toward staying single longer. This demographic trend shows the need for a new approach toward smaller abodes. Most single professionals don't need or want big houses and yards. So they tend to end up in condos or apartment buildings where there often isn't much individual expression or outdoor space. Tiny houses can offer an upscale environment with a small lawn and garden of your own without breaking the bank (and body) caring for a huge property.

Newlyweds

Let's face it, when you're in love you can't be too close to your sweetie — at least in the beginning. Thomas Jefferson felt just that. Beginning in 1770, he lived in a two-story 18-foot × 18-foot, 648-square-foot house with only 324 square feet per level. Mr. Jefferson used the main floor as a bedroom and office and the basement as a kitchen and living room.

Thomas Jefferson's honeymoon tiny house. This 648 square foot tiny home at Monticello (to the right in photo) is where Thomas Jefferson and his wife lived together for almost three years during Monticello's construction.

Thomas lived in his tiny home alone for about two years. Then he brought his bride Martha Wayles Skelton Jefferson to join him, and for three more years they lived together there while building Monticello. They called their tiny home the "honeymoon cottage."

Separated or Divorced People

In the United States the newest statistics from the Census Bureau show that married-couple households have slipped from 80 percent in the 1950s to less than 50 percent today. That translates to about 86 million single-adult heads of households. Unmarried adults make up about 42 percent of the workforce, 40 percent of home buyers, and 35 percent of registered voters.[1]

At the same time, more retired seniors are divorcing so they can qualify for Medicaid and receive higher monthly checks from Social Security. Others are living together without remarrying in order to avoid losing pensions or survivor health benefits that they have as widows or widowers.

Is it time to live on your own again? Need time and space to decide what to do about what isn't working anymore in your relationship or life? Tiny homes might be one viable solution.

Couples Who Make Better Neighbors than Housemates

There comes a time, especially in older partnerships, when lifestyles, eating habits, and sleeping patterns are, well, different. Each person has evolved more into their own identity, preferences, and patterns. Each one probably has different social and support groups. But the love and respect are still there.

One prominent and wealthy man was asked how he and his wife were still in a loving marriage of over 50 years. He said, "My wife and I are happily incompatible." How wonderful to acknowledge and accept that couples can be happy and grateful for their incompatibility instead of angry and blaming for their unique differences. To be happily incompatible about the things that set us apart and make us different. Accepting the issues we disagree on rather than blaming for failed expectations. Being thankful for each other. So why not be neighbors instead of housemates? You can be still close and supportive but far enough away to have your own life. You can be happily incompatible.

One of America's most respected actors, Katherine Hepburn, said it well: "Sometimes I wonder if men and women really suit each other. Perhaps they should live next door and just visit now and then." In other words, live close by and visit often.

Single Parents With (or Without) Kids

As a parent there may be times you simply need another bedroom or space of your own without the noise, clutter, and confusion of enthusiastic children. If you want your kids (and their friends) close but not in your face, check out tiny homes.

There are some parents who have their children with them only infrequently, maybe due to custody arrangements. A tiny home can be a very viable option for parents who have their children only part-time and therefore do not need a large space to maintain year round.

Nannies

Need more help with the kids? Is all that youthful energy too much to handle? How about a tiny home for a nanny to help with the little ones? Just put a tiny home in the backyard and make housing part of the nanny's pay plan and benefit package.

Physically Challenged People

One of our clients wanted her son in his own home yet close to her. We constructed a 500-square-foot tiny home in her backyard, without her having to buy an additional in-town lot. Everyone (and the dog) loves the living arrangement.

Fixed-Incomers

There is a growing number of baby boomers, retirees, and blue-collar workers who face living on a fixed income. No one knows if Social Security will be available ten years from now, especially with the current U.S. trillion-dollar deficit. Smaller homes can cost less to buy and maintain. It's that simple.

In-Betweeners

Crisis and conflict happen in all our lives. We are identifying as "in-betweeners" folks in transition from one life phase to another. Some life transitions are easier than others. We believe tiny houses can provide dignity and a new lease on life to these individuals by making decent housing available for them. Affordability is not always a necessary part of this equation. There are many affluent in-betweeners who also need self-esteem, support, and appropriate housing.

This 500-square-foot cottage was built for a patron in South Carolina for her son who is differently abled. This allows him to be nearby but have his own space.

Hermit-prone Individuals

Many of us just want to be left alone and live in our own space, to be still and quiet so we can connect with the divine, chat with our muse, and create our masterpieces, our gifts to the world ... or sleep.

Thoreau built his famous little cabin at Walden Pond. It was only 10 feet × 15 feet, 150 square feet. In his own words: "I went to the woods because I wished to live deliberately, to front only the essential facts of life and see if I could not learn what I had to teach and not, when I come to die, discover that I had not lived."

Everyone Else

Let's face it, any reason is good and any excuse is enough to justify a tiny home to call your own. Besides, it's politically correct, environmentally sensible, and economically sound. You deserve it.

Uses for Tiny Homes

We have described the types of people who might want to live in a tiny home. Now let's explore the many uses of tiny homes. We keep getting more clever ideas and living examples from folks across the country. Below are just a few ideas.

Extra Private Guest Rooms

Do you ever have guests you would like to see but don't want to live with? Good old snoring Uncle Joe, the smoking mother-in-law, your high school or army buddy who still hasn't matured, attention-deficit and out-of-control nephews, grumpy granddad, judgmental in-laws? We all have our cast of characters.

There are so many folks who want to see you and have some quality time together while they tour the country. Especially when they show up "for a week or so ... We'll see how long we'll stay..." Anyone in your life you can think of? Tiny houses might save many a relationship.

Starter Homes

A tiny home is great as a starter home that can be designed for future additions. Tiny homes can be designed specifically so that add-ons are easy and cost effective. For example, a window opening can be framed to become a future doorway leading to a new room. Additions can be built with only minor modifications as more space is needed and more money becomes available.

Student Housing

Put a tiny house, or a cluster of them, on an existing lot in your kid's college town. Then rent it to your genius offspring, and enjoy a tax write-off while they rent it. Upon graduation you can either sell the house or move it to a new location. This gives a cost-efficient place for the scholar to live and might have great resale value, a possible tax deduction, and real estate value appreciation for you.

Bed-and-Breakfast Expansion

Need an extra bedroom to rent out? Tiny homes offer a cost-effective and profitable way to add rooms without adding an expensive expansion of the main house. In many historic homes and districts it may not be possible to add on, but putting a tiny home out back may be perfectly acceptable. Be sure to check local zoning codes first.

Rental Income

Tiny homes can be rented, usually for the same as or more than premium efficiencies. They can be an easy way to generate passive income on land you already own. Wouldn't an extra $300 or more per month come in handy?

Home Office and Professional Space

Home office, professional space (massage, consultation, computer station) — do you need a separate place where you can work, concentrate, and keep your office intact without kids or other interference? Keep in mind, the current tax code allows 100 percent deduction for detached home offices.

Workshop for Hobbies, Pottery, Forge, Quilting, or Crafts

Almost everyone has a hobby or wants a special place to host those creative times. Tiny homes can be easily custom furnished with shelves and storage for all your art or hobby supplies. You can leave your projects in place without having to clean up for company.

Home Gym

All of us need to exercise, but sometimes the gym is too far or getting there too inconvenient. For the cost of a health club membership year after year you can have a home gym complete with a weight set, workout station, treadmill, mirrors, TV, music, even your own personal trainer.

Extended Home Care

A tiny home could house an extended-care giver such as a home-care nurse. This would give the caregiver an option of staying overnight in a nearby, yet private, space as well as allowing the patient to preserve their privacy. An intercom system between the two homes could help to monitor activity and needs.

Pout House

How many times have you just not wanted to go inside your house because you, or others, were angry and you knew there might be more tension and trouble? Everyone needs breathing space, time to reflect, and a safe, solitary space to do it once in a while. Pout houses provide escape.

Man Caves

John Gray, in his best-selling book *Men are from Mars and Women from Venus*, continually states that men need virtual "man caves" or secluded, private places where they can retreat. This means "No Trespassing" to anyone unless invited. Dr. Gray believes a man's need for his cave is the male's natural way of being. Such a cave is a place where he can deal with problems, putter, do guy things, and decorate as a man would. Some men use their cars or trucks as portable man caves, driving anywhere just to be alone with their thoughts. Others use garage workshops. We suggest tiny houses. Come to think of it, women often enjoy this sort of peaceful solitude as well. In fact, the name for them is "she sheds."

Away Space

Much in the same spirit as man caves and she sheds is the phrase coined by Sarah Susanka in her book *The Not So Big House* — "away space." This is a place of your own to use for whatever interests you. It might be your Friday night card game getaway, clay or art studio, hobby hut, writer's nook, meditation center, jig-saw puzzle workspace, or hideaway place to relax and regenerate.

Recreational and Vacation Getaways

Oh, those romantic cottages in the woods or next to a lake we all dream about. "Honey let's get away for a few days, just the two of us." You can often build or set tiny houses on sites where other houses might not be possible to build, such as your own fantasy island.

Retreat Centers with Private Cottages

There is a Buddhist center close by that uses tiny homes for their long-term students and others who are attending programs and workshops. The same could be true for corporate guests and staff housing, church camps, and vacation resorts.

Chapter 2

Tiny Homes Can Help You Have More Time, More Freedom, and More Money

W HO DOESN'T WANT TO HAVE MORE TIME, more free-dom, and more money in their lives?

Just the sheer size of the modern American dream home means that families often require two incomes, and sometimes even more, in order to pay the mortgage.

We have met dozens of families over the years who have complained about the lack of money to meet their standard of living, yet they fail to do the one thing that will almost guaran-tee they can live within their means, and that is to sell their big house and downsize to one that is more suited to their needs and income.

Granted, there are circumstances in which a larger home makes good sense; for example, if you have more people to share it with, or need extra rooms for your office, at-home business, artist studio, workspace, or workshop.

> I'm a slave to my house! Every weekend and all my spare time is eaten up by chores, lawn care, painting, repair, cleaning. These are sucking me dry! Is my life nothing more than just house maintenance?
>
> — Single mother with three kids who prefers to remain anonymous, British Columbia, Canada.

A larger home is needed for housing an extended family in a three-generation home. These were common into the 20th century, when three and sometimes even four generations shared a house. New housing designs can accommodate multi-generations with in-law apartments, granny flats, and teenager suites.

Yet, if you do not need a large home to house many people, a tiny home can help you reevaluate how to spend your time and money and can directly affect the amount of freedom in your life.

You can take pride in learning how much is enough and in accepting the freedom of voluntary simplicity. In the end you will have a smaller number of quality things that serve you rather than a large number of things that own you.

There is an element of self-esteem, self-sufficiency, pride, and independence that can come with living in a smaller home. It's an inner power rather than a display of external trappings. It's self-knowing. It's being rich by having enough. It's wealth by contentment.

In the U.S. today, placing such emphasis on the size of one's home has taken on the ugly connotation that if you live in a large house then you are successful and a good provider. Conversely, if you live in a small home you are often thought of as being inferior or poorer than those who live in a big house. From that view, anyone could get an inferiority complex from such narrow thinking.

Authentic power is not wrapped up in external items we often get for show and to impress others. A big paycheck doesn't have to translate into a big house and lots of things. You cannot buy true self-esteem.

How a Tiny Home Can Promote an Improved Way of Life

+ Smaller mortgage payments than for a big home (although some tiny homes sell for over $200,000!).
+ Lower property taxes, generally.
+ Less space to heat or cool year after year — this saves you big bucks on heating and air conditioning bills.
+ Less need for electricity, as tiny homes tend to have fewer rooms with more natural lighting. They tend not to need so much artificial light.

+ Building a new tiny house can save you big bucks because it takes fewer building materials, less energy, and less labor than larger homes. This also helps conserve the Earth's ecology, forests, and non-renewable resources.
+ Less construction time. It takes much less time to build a 1,000-square-foot house than it does a 3,000-square-foot house. This saves on construction loan interest and decreases rental time and/or mortgage payment on your previous residence.
+ You can achieve financial independence faster by paying down a smaller mortgage, lowering property taxes, and having smaller continuing monthly utility and maintenance expenses. We define financial independence as when passive income (income from investments, rentals, royalties) is equal to or greater than your expenses.

> Authentic power is not wrapped up in external items we often get for show and to impress others. A big paycheck doesn't have to translate into a big house and lots of things. You cannot buy true self-esteem.

+ Travel. Leaving a smaller house for weeks or months needs much less preparation, cleaning, or consideration compared to larger houses. Set the thermostat on minimum and save money on heating or air conditioning while you travel.
+ Fewer visitors. We built a tiny home for a lady who didn't want visitors. She built small specifically to keep relatives from mooching off her. She was tired of cooking and entertaining live-in guests. This may or may not give you more time, freedom, and money, but it might save on grocery bills and cooking time for guests. Tiny homes as guest houses are popular so you can have folks visit without sacrificing your own space ... but that might lead to more guests. It's a lifestyle question.
+ Fewer worries. If something really goes wrong with your house, when a disaster strikes (hurricane, tornado, flood, fire) then you don't have as much to lose as you do with a big house.

Repairs (roof replacement, window replacement, siding repairs) cost less and can be done much more quickly.

+ Smaller is easier to clean. This is a real no-brainer. Fewer windows to wash and less square footage to vacuum.

In many tiny homes you can vacuum the house without having to plug the sweeper in over and over. This is true in my home. My former 24-foot × 30-foot Lindal Cedar home in Virginia had the footprint of a two-car garage. I would leave the sweeper plugged in, sitting in the hallway corner. To vacuum the entire 720-square-foot downstairs kitchen, living room, office, and bath took me about seven minutes without changing plugs. The wood floors and oriental carpets make vacuuming go quickly.

Eight Ways You Can Save Money by Building a Tiny Home

1. Land Preparation. One of the first ways you can save money is on land preparation. It is entirely possible to build one of these little houses on piers that are dug by hand or with a post-hole digger attachment on a farm tractor.

2. Fewer Building Materials. A second big way we can save money with a tiny house is in the overall cost of the building materials. It simply does not take that many boards, nails, windows, and doors to build an honest little house.

3. Small Appliances. Appliances don't have to be full-size or extraordinarily expensive. Even if you add an energy-efficient washer and dryer you can buy all the appliances you need for less than the full-sized versions.

4. Smaller Heating and Cooling Systems. In many instances you won't need central heating and air conditioning. You can get by very nicely with a small vented propane fireplace for heat and a window air conditioner for cooling, especially if you have designed and situated your little house

to take advantage of passive solar heating and cooling. In a more elaborate scenario you can use a through-the-wall heat pump, which both heats and cools, depending on your needs. For someone who really wants to have the feel of a warm home, a small woodburning stove with a glass front that allows you to see the flames is a nice touch. We prefer to elevate the wood stove approximately two feet in order to have storage beneath and so we have a more direct view of the flames.

5. Smaller Bathroom(s). Since you will probably have only one bathroom, you can splurge a bit on the fixtures. Instead of just an ordinary tub, you can look at putting in one of the whirlpool tubs, and justify the cost as well-body maintenance. A soothing whirlpool bath can do wonders for massaging sore and aching muscles and for relieving stress.

6. Outdoor Shower. You might also consider adding an outdoor shower for use in the warmer weather. There is something positively energizing about a hot shower in the open air with the sun or moon shining down. A stylish enclosure made with decay-resistant wood can be very attractive and pleasing.

7. Safe DIY Home Maintenance. Because your tiny house will be only one or two stories high, you may be more courageous to climb up and do the maintenance chores that you might otherwise have to hire someone else to do on a full-size house, for example, cleaning gutters, washing windows, or painting the house.

8. Less Painting Inside and Out. Painting is much easier and faster on a tiny house — and practically painless if you only do one side each year. Cleaning gutters, trimming shrubs, tending flowers in the window boxes, all require much less of your time when the house is smaller and has fewer shrubs and window boxes.

Chapter 3

Real Life Examples of Tiny Homes and the People Who Love Them

OVER THE YEARS we have built several different styles of tiny houses, and each one has a unique story behind it. Below are descriptions of just a few tiny homes and the people who love them.

※彡❀彡※

Case Study 1: Terri Bsullak's Tiny Home

We built a single-story tiny house, measuring 20 feet × 30 feet (600 square feet) that cost around $35,000 to build. As a single woman and social services worker, Terri found a tiny home affordable and all she wanted.

Terri's house has a large living room/dining area/kitchen measuring 20 feet × 20 feet, and a bedroom and bath area measuring 20 feet × 10 feet.

Features that make Terri's cottage so perfect for her are:

Terri Bsullak.

- Six hundred square feet — just enough space for one person, or two people who really get along
- One bedroom (with a futon in the living room that can be a guest bed when needed)

- Basic and simple open floor plan
- Rainwater harvesting, storage, and filtration
- Direct vent gas space heater with a wood stove backup
- Lots of windows for natural sunlight and air flow
- Metal roof for longevity and rainwater harvesting
- Plywood siding that looks like traditional board and batten
- Ramp instead of steps to the front door

Terri's determination to achieve her ideal living space can be an inspiration to us all. She tells us how in her own words.

I wasn't planning on buying or building my own house — until my landlords got a divorce. I then had to figure out what to do next. I initially thought I had to find another place to rent. The place was perfect. A small cottage that I was renting from friends. It was inexpensive and out in the county. As I began to look around at other places to rent, I realized it wasn't very easy to find what I wanted.

Someone suggested I buy a house. I said no. I felt there was no way I could. I didn't have a down payment. I felt I just couldn't afford to do that. Then I started looking around at different mortgage companies and one of them said that they could probably get me a mortgage for around $25,000. I almost cried, because I knew that wasn't going to buy a house.

I finally got another mortgage company to help me out with reducing some of my other bills, student loans, and monthly expenses; I qualified!

I started looking around at places to buy, and I knew I couldn't do a lot of the fixer-uppers that were in my price range. It was very difficult looking and looking and looking. I would find a place and think it might be a possibility, and then it was sold already. Then someone suggested that I build. I initially thought I'd never do that. I had never lived in a brand-new house before. And then, at some point I was reading the newspaper, and there was an article about Andy and Pat's Tiny House Company. And I thought, Yes. That's perfect! That's what I need!

I am small myself. At the time I had a small car, a Mazda Miata. I've since traded my little Miata for a compact pickup truck. I didn't need anything bigger. I rebel against America's attitude in general, about the bigger the better. I am appalled at the lifestyle of people who need big steaks and big houses and big everything.

> It wasn't that I wanted a tiny house just because I thought it would be inexpensive. I just like small things.
>
> — Terri Bsullak

I had traveled to Europe and different places where bigger is not better all the time. They have these beautiful small cars, small roads, small houses, and it is wonderful. Bigger is not better. Bigger is detrimental in so many cases. I didn't want anything huge to clean, and all the different reasons including my commitment to our environment.

I have been involved with the Greens over the years. I am a vegetarian, and a lot of environmental issues are important to me. Why make it harder for the environment and the population in general by having huge everything? I wondered if I could afford a tiny house. And if I could afford a tiny house, then what about finding a piece of land?

It was a huge challenge to try to find something that I could afford. I was thinking perhaps two acres in the county. But no, after looking, I couldn't even find that. Little pieces of land were difficult to find, and the places that I found that were in my price range were just awful pieces of land, like being cliffside, or having to cross the river three times to access. They were situations that I just couldn't manage.

Finally this realtor friend had a piece of land for sale. It was much more land than I wanted: 22 acres. He suggested that maybe I could divide it up, split it with somebody. I saw the land and I decided that I just had to have it to myself. I got greedy once I saw it. So I switched things around. I had a certain amount that I was going to spend for the land, and a certain amount to spend for the house. I paid a little bit more for the land, a little less for the house. I felt if I could swing that, then I could actually make it happen.

The situation with the land was challenging. I needed to get a right-of-way through the neighbor's land, trees had to be cleared, and a driveway had to be built. Pretty much everyone I spoke to told me I was crazy for trying to build on that land. But I was determined. Yet with all the problems, the purchase of the land happened very quickly. There were many setbacks, but I decided that I was going to make it happen. And now every single day, I just say to myself, "this is my little house, and I created it and I love it."

Having been in my home for over a year, I just can't imagine what I would do differently. I am not thinking it would be nicer to have more space or have this or that. There's nothing that I would change. It's absolutely perfect. Last week I had some friends come up who hadn't seen the house, and there were eight of us here. At first I was worried about having enough space because it is a tiny house, but everyone had places to sit down, and they were comfortable. They loved it. It was a lot of fun, and we enjoyed each other's company.

My total home is 20 feet × 30 feet (600 square feet). When you first walk in, the big main room and kitchen is 20 feet × 20 feet (400 square feet), so it doesn't seem like a tiny house.

It doesn't seem small at all. I have lots of windows, it's open and bright. I definitely like my light above my sink. I don't like having a light on in the middle of the day, so I think the placement of windows is critical.

My home has high ceilings, which gives the feeling of spaciousness. It has a tiny little bedroom and a tiny little bathroom. It was a long process to get the design that I wanted that would work. I had some ideas, but I didn't know if they would work until Andy Lee of the Tiny House Company helped me figure that out. We came up with the design in the end that just worked out perfectly. I have my sliding glass doors looking out onto my deck and forest.

Wood is my main heat, but I do have a direct vent propane heater that I can use. It doesn't take a lot to heat my house, it's so small. The refrigerator is electric. My kitchen cabinets, bathroom vanity, and all the interior doors were handmade by Andy and they came out beautifully. It is so much fun to show it off to people.

It also was wonderful that Andy let me do some of the work. I did the painting. I feel that I got to know the house because I've actually painted every inch of it.

I love my wood floors. A friend and I installed them ourselves in two days. They don't show dirt and are easily cleaned.

My deck is divine. It is 8 feet × 8 feet (only 164 square feet) — small, but perfect for me. I spend hours and hours sitting out there. I take my food, my knitting, and my books out to enjoy the outdoors. And I love to sit outside to work and think, so even at nine at night during the summer, I'm still sitting outside.

My kitchen is designed so that I don't have to walk just to get to the stove from the refrigerator. I have a friend who has a huge kitchen. I don't like cooking in her kitchen because it is so big and I have to walk so much.

It's too much work to cook; too much walking! Totally inefficient! For me especially, big spaces can be quite a problem because of the way I walk.

⚜

One of the reasons that everyone at Tiny House Company so admires Terri is that she has a disability, but she is one of the last people anyone would think of as disabled. Terri has a cyst on her spinal cord that prevents her from walking normally. But it doesn't slow her down from skiing, hiking, canoeing, or accomplishing her dreams, including her tiny dream home.

I have known Terri for years. She looks healthier than most people I know. Terri's eyes have a light in them. She has a big, healthy, genuine smile. She is the ideal weight, has great muscle tone, and has clear skin. She is physically fit and energetic. Terri is unstoppable and is a positive thinker and inspiration to us all.

⚜

A lot of people think I shouldn't be living alone because I walk with a limp and fall down a lot. I have a hard time getting up stairs, but falling doesn't bother me as much as it does others. I am determined to be in a space that I love, and I love my tiny home. My "disability" just makes me stronger.

I also want to say that I definitely recommend my ramp instead of stairs. It is something that I use every day, and I forget how special it is. It

Terri Bsullak in her kitchen/living room/office. The open floor plan lets her use the space for multiple purposes, and the hand-crafted, knotty pine cabinets give a custom look. Terri's very efficient floor plan was designed by Andy Lee, co-owner of Tiny House Company. The large living room/dining room/ kitchen measures 20 feet × 20 feet. The bedroom and bath area is 20 feet × 10 feet.

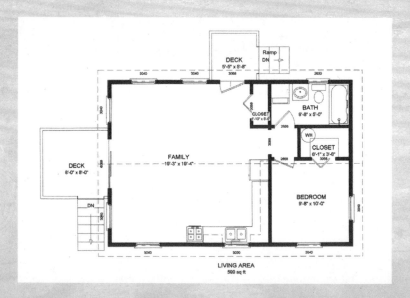

blends with the whole house, and it doesn't look weird. It's so much easier for me to get into my house. It is also a treat to be able to invite others over who have accessibility challenges. For example, I have a friend who uses a wheelchair and many other friends who have physical challenges.

The word we use is "visit-ability," and that word means a lot to us who are "differently enabled."

My ramp makes it possible to have friends with disabilities come to my house. There are so few houses in the county that they can get into at all. My ramp adds richness to my life that I hadn't considered before.

The old house that I rented before had three or four nice beautiful stone steps, but its visit-ability factor was zero. I had to get up them without a railing. I pretty much fell every time. I never fall on my ramp at my new house. It's a wonderful asset for me and my friends. Andy Lee knew. He just put it in without asking me. When I drove up and first saw it I knew immediately it was perfect. I cried out of joy.

At first, rainwater harvesting was totally out of the question for Terri. She didn't want to hear about It. However, Terri was forced to do rainwater harvesting off her roof or not live in her house.

I thought I had to have a conventional well. My well driller has a lot of experience, but after spending over five weeks and drilling five dry holes at over 300 feet each, we had to give up. We kept hitting caves and ledge. I paid him $6,000 for dry holes — and that was half price!

Andy Lee finally convinced me to try rainwater harvesting. I had no other choice if I was going to live in my tiny home; and there was nothing more in the world I wanted than my own home. So I was motivated to be open to any possibility.

My rainwater collection system was not expensive. It cost $800 for gutters, roof washer, and connecting to my cistern. The cistern cost $2,500 which included installation, pump, and connection to the house. So for $3,200 I have water!

> Rainwater harvesting is so natural. The rain falls and I have water, direct from the source. What could be simpler? In hindsight, I don't know why I was so hesitant to do rainwater harvesting.
>
> — Terri Bsullak

This year there has been so much rain that I have too much for my holding tank. But that's not a problem, it just drains out as it would without my rain harvesting system.

During the drought I had water delivered, but it cost only $30 for a thousand gallons. That's no big deal. I don't use as much water as most people. My cistern holds enough for a three-month supply, so with one water delivery, I had three months of water. That's cheaper than most people pay for city water in one month. I love it!

From the Tiny House Company's view, as contractors, there is a lot more joy for us building a tiny house for someone like Terri than in building a larger house for people who don't really appreciate it. We make more money building bigger houses, but it takes lots longer and is often not worth our time.

Terri's house has given her a new lease on life. She is so proud of her little house and has put love into all the details that make her little home a unique and beautiful expression of her.

For me, of all people, to make building and owning my own home happen is amazing. Tiny House Company helped me make it happen. I was able to get a loan and able to buy 22 acres and everything. Professionally, I am a mental health and substance abuse counselor with the county. I had been working as a counselor for only about two years before deciding to build my new home. I wasn't making much money at all. I also was paying off my student loans from when I went to graduate school to get a Master's in Social Work. Before graduate school, I was working and traveling for ten years and pretty much survived on ten thousand dollars a year.

If I were to give advice to someone considering a tiny house, I would say, "Just do it." Several people that I know are considering building a house, and I invite them to come up and see my home. It will show them that they can do it, too! It's great.

This photo shows the backside of Terri's house and her beloved deck. Note the gutter at the right of the house leading to a cistern for rainwater harvesting. The front of the house with the ramp leading to the front door is on the other side.

Case Study 2: The Lanes' Shed Home

Howard and Barbara Lane

As builders, it's not just about money for us, although we have to make a fair profit. Building and promoting tiny homes is also about making a cultural difference in what we, as a society, value in housing.

— Patricia Foreman

Barbara and Howard Lane have a lot of experience living in small places. Barbara grew up on a bay on Lake Ontario where many people she knew and played with lived in compact quarters, both on boats and in small cottages.

Howard was a career naval officer. From his years on boats he appreciated the finer nuances of living in small quarters. After he retired they put everything into storage and traveled across the U.S., living in a van for almost a year.

Their travels in their Dodge utility van gave them an even finer appreciation of how to utilize space in a way that nothing else could. Their little home on wheels had only 72 square feet of space. It's not that this was a small couple, either. Howard was a commanding 6'4" and Barbara an impressive and fit 5'10".

After their van travels they bought 215 gorgeous acres in the Blue Ridge Mountains and built a 4,000-square-foot house, which they had planned as a retreat center. But first, they built a 12-foot × 16-foot tiny garden house (192 square feet) to stay in and to store tools in while working on their 4,000-square-foot big house. Over the several years of building their big house, they lived full time in the garden shed and grew to appreciate the cozy, safe, and organized lifestyle their tiny house offered. They have offices, hobby space, bathrooms, and a kitchen in the big house, but spend most of their alone time in the tiny house.

Here is Barbara's story.

Growing up, I lived right across from a yacht club, so a lot of the people I knew lived on boats and had little tiny cottages, maybe 16 feet × 16 feet (256 square feet), that included a kitchen, a living room, and a bedroom. These were very informal summer cottages, and the owners spent a lot of time outdoors.

And some of the people I knew converted sail lockers into living spaces for the summer. So they would have a living area, maybe 12 feet × 12 feet (144 square feet), and half this space above would be a loft where they would sleep in sleeping bags. They would cook outdoors, and they would use the yacht club showers and bathrooms, and they would hang out outdoors. Although they lived in these tiny spaces, the club itself had big, big living areas, so if anyone wanted more space for the day they could always go down to the club, or they could sit outside on the covered porches.

> While living in such small places, there isn't necessarily a clear distinction between being inside and being outside. You live your life as if it is a picnic. I love it.
>
> — Barbara Lane

Even while growing up I would study boats in order to plan tiny houses, because the way a boat is engineered and the way the space is used is totally different than in a typical house. This has been a passion for me all my life. I cooked outdoors for many years, and one of the things that I discovered was a "cowboy kitchen." I fell in love with the cowboy kitchen. It was a unit that the cowboys would take on rides or fence mending. It wasn't really a wagon where they could cook inside; it was a semi-permanent unit, and they could close up the counter against the shelves. They also had rodent proofing on it. It was wonderful. It was so funky and practical.

Sometimes these cowboy kitchens were just out there, in the middle of nowhere. Sometimes they were on wagons, and they would haul them. That was the model for my outdoor kitchen. For nearly seven years, I cooked outdoors in a 6-foot × 12-foot (72-square-foot) area covered by a tarp.

Barbara Lane standing in front of her tiny house. The door to the left originally had a refrigerator, but now it has a kiln for firing Barbara's pottery. The outdoor "cowboy kitchen" is to the right and has a brick floor that wraps around the house.

In the winter time I cooked inside the garden shed on a single-burner propane stove. I also used an electric frying pan, a microwave, and a toaster oven. I still do. In the early days I had a Coleman stove, and now I have a big, commercial-size cooker with a grill in my cowboy kitchen, but I still often cook inside on a single burner.

When we first moved into the cabin it was meant to be temporary. We had spent two winters in the neighbor's small cabin, and it was much bigger than this, maybe four times bigger. It had a bathroom and closets. But we got tired of commuting back and forth so we decided to spend the third winter here and live in the shed on our own land. We insulated it and added a woodburning stove, even though it took up a lot of floor space.

As we spent more and more time in that shed I decided I preferred the feeling of comfort, safety, and accessibility that the shed offered compared

Barbara Lane in her cowboy kitchen. Notice how the pantry has a fold-up shelf that doubles as counter space and, when folded up, keeps everything clean and bug and rodent proof. There is a ceiling fan and light that makes this a wonderful area in which to sit in the rocking chair and visit with the cook. The firewood is for the woodstove inside.

to the expanse of our big home. We moved into our 4,000-square-foot home for a period of a few weeks. I found the large space to be at times spooky and not nearly as relaxing and cozy as our tiny home.

So now our 4,000-square-foot home is the equivalent of my childhood yacht club. That's where the socializing takes place, where the groups can gather, and where I can sprawl. But for everyday living, the 12-foot × 16-foot garden shed was our choice! We continued to live in this tiny little garden shed since 1996. Since Howard died two years ago, I am now living alone, and I am even more attracted to living in the smaller space.

This photo shows both of the Lane houses to give you an idea of their location relative to each other: the 192-square-foot tiny house is in the foreground and the 4,000-square-foot house behind it. They are about 200 feet from each other. You can also see Barbara's outdoor cowboy kitchen on the left and solar shower to the right and the insulated stainless steel woodstove chimney in the center of the tiny house. Note the skylights in the patio/cowboy kitchen area that let in natural light.

❦

Barbara has found through experience that there are necessary tricks to living in tiny spaces. When asked what she would do differently, Barbara states that if she were to modify her cabin she would add a bathroom.

❦

I have used what I call my bathroom bucket buddy during much of my tiny house living experience. When Howard and I were traveling in our van we routinely used a five-gallon plastic bucket at night. Even when we were staying with friends and sleeping in the van it was more convenient than going inside and possibly waking everyone up. Bucket bathrooms are also very common among Peace Corps volunteers overseas. They are very practical.

In many ways our van traveling was our first tiny-house experience — only on wheels. We learned the necessity of organization and the efficiency of proper space utilization.

Further tricks to living in tiny spaces include custom building and using a cupboard that is on wheels. I can move it depending on what I'm doing. I've learned to have and use furniture that serves multiple functions.

When we first moved into the shed, we had two extra-long twin beds that we slept on. We used these beds as a sofa as well as a bed. And as we went along we decided, hey, we are here longer than we thought, and we decided that we would like to sleep together. We modified it so that we had a twin bed and a queen-size bed. In between the beds is a tiny little shelf, probably five inches wide. Just enough for an arm rest or to set a cup of tea. It's almost like a centerboard on a boat. It fits between the two beds, and only takes up a half-inch of floor space. And then Howard built in shelf after shelf after shelf after shelf.

I suggest building furniture, such as cabinetry, to the sizes that fit your needs specifically. I also suggest maximizing the use of space down to the nearest quarter inch. Howard and I had long discussions about a quarter inch here, a quarter inch there. It can make such a difference in how the space feels. Everything in our shed is well thought out and carefully measured. The spice rack is just tall enough for the spices; the tea shelf is just tall enough for two boxes of tea, and so on. We have custom shelves for specific purposes. Very precise and efficient.

I also suggest that anyone considering living in a tiny house give thought to natural light, ventilation, ceiling height, heating options, and insulation. All the things that one wants in a regular-size house. You can do a lot with very little. I suggest that you extend your space into the

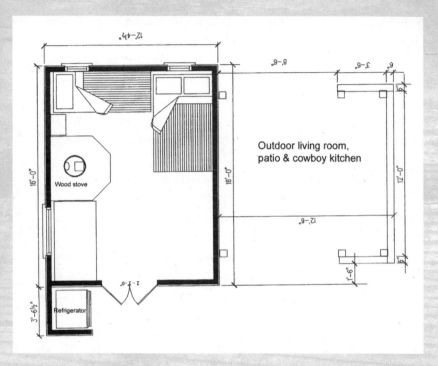

The Lanes' tiny home floor plan includes a twin and double bed, woodstove, and kitchen counter.

outdoors, such as an outdoor patio for cooking and dining when the weather permits.

❧

Barbara goes on to explain her philosophy about living in tiny houses.

❧

I don't live in my tiny house because it's upscale or anything practical. I can afford anything I want. I live in my tiny house because it's magic. It's a different magical world.

Conventional, modern, modular houses don't involve much of anything that is handcrafted. They all have the same plastic, void look and the feel that is impersonal, mass produced — drywall and plastic. At best, people make it theirs with curtains and wall art, but it's still mass produced and homogenized. There is not much you can do to change that feeling, that dull, uninspiring ambiance.

In tiny houses the rules of civilized living shift. It's okay to put your feet up. It's okay to be casual and yourself. As an analogy, you are playing a different game living in a tiny house. In an ordinary house you are playing Monopoly. In a tiny house you are playing Hobbit.

This might sound abstract but I also get the sense about the outside "body of air" being closer in a tiny house. I'm not sure how to explain it, but just like in a boat there is water all around, very close, and that has a certain feeling and has a certain energy; it's the same with air in a tiny house. You are not very far from the outside body of air. In big buildings that have offices sandwiched between offices or hotel rooms stacked all around, there is, for me, a closed in and very different quality to the air. The outside is more removed. Some hotels try to compensate for this with big atriums and water fountains, but it's still not the same. Tiny homes put you closer to the outside air and all that is happening within your immediate climate and environment. I like that.

There is something about miniaturization that appeals to people. Senses and imagination expand. In a tiny house you set your perception at a different level. Magical things happen. Our culture really doesn't have the vocabulary to describe living in tiny houses. The best we come up with is cozy, but it's way beyond cozy. I hope Patricia and Andy with this Tiny Homes book can help develop a vocabulary to describe the pure and simple delight of living in tiny homes and special places.

I am a fanatic about tiny homes. I think most people love them. It comes from childhood; something primal within us. Everyone has fun memories or fantasies about playhouses and tree houses. Those special magical places that are safe from the outside world. I think they're wonderful. I just love them.

— Barbara Lane

Barbara is a retired mathematician, counselor, and master potter, among her many skills. After Howard passed away the big house was too much for her alone, so she sold the property and moved to

As a potter and an artist, I am very clear that I want to live a handcrafted life. I also want to live in a handcrafted house. I create it. My house and I are unique in all the world. We become expressions of each other.

— Barbara Lane

Vermont to be close to her twin grandsons. She found a place that allows her have a pottery studio and some rentals. Yet she continues to retain that feeling of a tiny home in an apartment she designed for herself.

Barbara Lane in her tiny house. The two beds, a queen and a single, double as couches. Note that all the bookshelves have keepers (tiny arms that latch around the front) so that if there is ever an earthquake the books won't fall. This way of keeping items in place is common in boats. The TV (lower right corner) is positioned for viewing from the beds.

Case Study 3: Ray Pealer's Tiny House Trade Station

In the words of Ray Pealer:

A few years ago, my wife and I chose to change our lifestyle and to take some chances in order to go after our dreams. She had just given birth to a baby girl, and we wanted to experience with her such things as clean air, natural surroundings, and a healthy community.

We decided that we would sell our house and make the transition from a suburban residence to a cottage or cabin in the mountains. We gave the house a fresh coat of paint, put it up for sale, moved our things into a storage unit, and set off on the road for a new place to call home. After driving all over the region, we found a cabin rental in the Catskill Mountains of New York. It was for us a perfectly sized space of about 700

Ray and his daughter in his Tiny Homes 300-square-foot New England-style cottage, which he uses as his work-at-home day trading station.

square feet, which sat on a quiet street and was surrounded by forest. Our house got an offer and then sold while we moved into the rented cabin in the woods.

We felt blessed to be living out our dreams. During the days my wife took care of our daughter as I worked out of the second bedroom with my fledgling business of day trading. This went well for about the first month or so. Then, in what seemed overnight, our delightful little girl went from squirming and crawling to walking and then running. Inevitably, she would leave the area of activity at the other end of the house and make a beeline through the house for my door. In my life, there have been few things more difficult than ignoring my beautiful little baby girl as she pleaded "dada" from the other side of the door. Despite my wife's best efforts to play defense, put up blockades, create distractions, it was a losing battle. The stress was taking over.

We explored our options, but given the rural location and that we were only renting the little place, they seemed pretty limited. What made the process even more difficult was that we had grown quite fond of our cabin rental. We loved the warm wood interior surfaces, crackling fireplace, and cheery, open floor plan. What lay outside was just as wonderful. Winter brought a fresh blanket of snow to the familiar landscape, the forest was incredibly quiet, and we had grown to love this gorgeous haven.

It was the middle of the winter, so the few options present in a rural area were even more limited. There was first the idea of moving to a larger rental with a studio space, but they were few and far between and quite costly as well. Renting a separate studio for the business was also expensive, and nothing was advertised locally. What could we do?

The last thing we wanted to do was to move back into town and risk losing the woodsy lifestyle just so we could have one quiet room with a desk.

If we did rent an office space away from home, we would have additional costs of rent and commuting, and I would have had less time both at home and at the office. My work as a day trader is composed of large blocks of high-intensity time broken up by expanses of less intense focus. Together these blocks of time span from 7 a.m. to 10 p.m. I knew that if I was off-site, I would be making multiple trips back and forth to home throughout the day, or I would spend the entire day away from home, or my work would suffer if I abbreviated my tasks. It made financial and logistical sense to be on the site, and the calculations proved that constructing or bringing in an additional structure would be the ideal way to go, especially considering the potential tax benefits of having a stand-alone home office.

As we digested these concepts, I stayed up several nights drawing out an idea for a mobile office design. The final design came about from concentrating on what we really needed until it became absolutely clear. It started as a shed, changed into an RV, went back to a shed on wheels, and then finally morphed into something more than all combined. It was a cottage on wheels. Looking somewhat impractical at first, as I shaved off some of the mass, it shaped into the perfect size.

The design now complete, I wondered if someone else had already thought of this. After days of surfing all over the web, I was scanning through eBay, searching for something wooden within the RV section. It was one of those moments when you are so close and have been working so hard that you are about to give up. I decided to scan down through all the RVs again, and there at the bottom was a little house on wheels. I remember the feeling when I saw it. I wasn't surprised. It just was there, and it was right.

I made arrangements with the Tiny House Company to purchase and pick up a tiny, ready-to-go cottage unit. I was incredibly excited about how quickly this idea's time had come. Seeing the house for the first time, I was even more impressed. It was spacious for its size, thanks to a cathedral ceiling and a loft above. I towed it home, and my landlord helped pull it into the snow-covered yard with his truck. I leveled it and had power connected just in time, just before the coming storm. The next week, while the temperature dropped below zero and the snow piled up, I enjoyed the cozy, silent space. At first it was strange not having any interruptions, but soon I became used to working with the luxury of complete concentration. Now I cannot imagine ever going without it. I consider it one of the best decisions we've made.

My commute takes all of a minute; sometimes it doubles if I need to take another trip to carry breakfast. My wife and I came up with a schedule so we both know when I will be available. I can now dedicate the long periods of concentration necessary for computerized stock trading and can reduce my stress by being in such a peaceful spot. The best part is, I can take off during the daylight hours to spend delightful, uninterrupted time with my daughter and my wife.

A wise friend of mine, when he heard about this new improvement to our backyard, chuckled and said, "Every man needs his cave." I agree. This space allows me to think, process, and meditate not just on work but the other things in life as well. I find that I handle life with much more grace as a result of having a place of solitude.

This decision to have a tiny office on wheels keeps our office costs low, gives me a comfortable work environment, and I can continue to be part of the family while having the necessary autonomy.

— Ray Pealer

Meanwhile, my family continues to enjoy life amidst our beautiful, natural surroundings. We take walks, study the plants, and enjoy this rare place. Our daughter loves to scamper about the woods, picking up and investigating everything she finds. She laughs as she plays in the streams nearby, and listens with concern to the wind when it comes through the forest. She has met little friends with whom she can share her early years, and we've entered into a community of families with similar aspirations.

We're thankful that we are able to give these experiences to her and to ourselves. We're also especially thankful that the Tiny House Company had the insight to produce these little homes so that we can continue realizing our dreams.

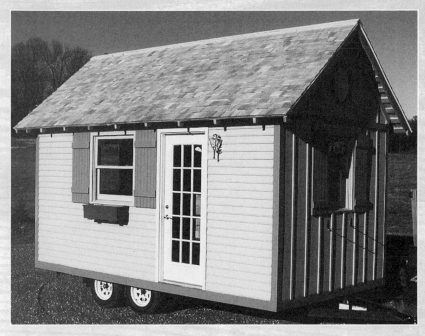

The tiny cabin, called "Tiny Grey," built by Tiny House Company, now serves as Ray's home office. This tiny cabin offers handcrafted style with lots of light, handmade shutters, and a cozy interior of knotty pine walls and hardwood flooring.

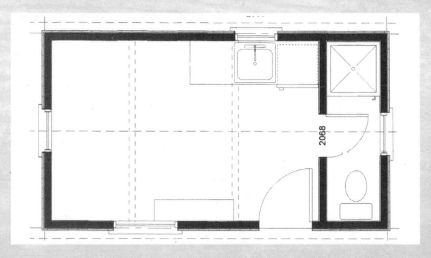

Case Study 4: The Campbells' Combined Workshop and Garden Shed — Call It Anything But a House

Danny and Cindy Campbell

Danny and Cindy Campbell contracted with the Tiny House Company to build a 450-square-foot tiny house "shed" in their backyard to use for hobbies. Cindy's passion is her gardens and landscaping, and she keeps their house and grounds looking like the feature home in a national garden tour. Danny loves woodworking and the various projects Cindy lovingly assigns him.

They both work full-time jobs. Danny Campbell is the warehouse manager at Spencer's Home Center, and Cindy is the manager of The Palms, a popular restaurant in downtown Lexington, Virginia. They are in their 40s and their kids, Heather and Jessie, have left home to build their own lives. Their 1,300-square-foot ranch home just didn't have the space they always wanted for a garden shed and workshop. In Cindy's words:

We simply needed more hobby space, that's why we had the tiny house built. I call it my garden shed, and Danny calls it his workshop. And as far as sharing the space, the line down the middle is much more my side than his. We have a little storage building that is quite a distance from our house, and it is just too far, too small, and too dark. I worked out of our basement for a while with my gardening, but it was so dark and drab it really didn't inspire me.

For so long I really wanted to have a garden shed with lots of light. A place that enticed me to come out and work in it. I put in such long hours at the restaurant, and gardening is my therapy. I can be very stressed after work. When I go out into the garden shed I forget everything that has bothered me during the day. It's a whole other world — an inward soul thing.

※≈◎≈※

I first met Cindy while taking Master Gardener classes together. I understand how Cindy's garden shed is like a little chapel for her. It is her sacred place, where she can be by herself with her plants and musings, and commune with nature in her own quiet space. I am surprised that Cindy is not a professional landscape designer, because her lawn and gardens are so beautiful. Andy has known Danny for several years through buying lumber at Spencer Home Center.

The design for the shed was partly driven by some gorgeous circle-top custom windows that a customer had special ordered and returned to Spencer's Home Center. Being the warehouse manager, Danny got a great deal on them.

※≈◎≈※

This photo shows the front of the Campbell tiny house with the circle-top windows and stone foundation.

Inside the Campbells' garden/workshop tiny house with the open, high ceilings and exposed beams. Cabinets and plenty of shelves provide organized storage and make an excellent use of space. The circle-top windows add lots of natural light, passive solar heat, and stylishness.

Danny designed our garden shed to take the best advantage of the windows. The style of the shed really matches the style of our house. The roof pitch and the color — it's like it has been here all along.

Even though the tiny house is small, it is a good size compared to our house. The tiny house is designed very well, allowing lots of natural light. The high vaulted, tongue-and-groove pine ceilings also add charm and character to the house.

I was initially hesitant about putting it so close to the main house, but Danny pointed out that the distance was one of the complaints that we have about the other building on our property. It was very important to me that the shed style flow with the house, being that it was so close.

For us the design is really good, because although we share the shed, Danny has his space and I have mine. It gives us something that we can

> I think people stay more connected when they are in smaller surroundings. It kept our family close. In a small home you interact more; you have to. You are together, you talk, play, communicate, and share ideas. I think that is very, very important in life.
>
> — Cindy Campbell

do in the winter when we really can't get out in the yard. We can share the same space and it is very well organized. We can each be in our own little world, yet we can be there together while we are working on our own projects. These are the times when we kick back ideas about the projects that we want to do. I always have a project.

※※◎※※

Danny feels this way about his creation:

※※◎※※

I don't think there is anything that I would have done differently in our garden shed. We could use heat and air conditioning, but that will probably come in time. We just really didn't want to spend the money, and a little space heater warms it up quickly. I am really happy with the way that it is.

We gave a lot of thought to the planning of our shed. The windows make it seem very spacious. I wanted lots of light.

My advice to anyone considering building a shed is "Don't make the mistake of putting it too far away from your house. You won't use it." Our shed was a neat project. Tiny buildings such as garden sheds are fun, and the hobby space has added a new dimension to our lives.

※※◎※※

Cindy states:

※※◎※※

It will be warm enough in the shed so that it will be a little mini-hothouse. A great place to grow my plants. I plan to take advantage of that next spring. We love our shed. I can sit on my side of the shed and watch the birds, and they have no clue that I am there.

※※◎※※

In discussing tiny and small houses in general, both Danny and Cindy feel that raising their family in a small home had huge advantages and helped them stay together as a close-knit family.

Case Study 5: Uncle Gene's Tiny Shed Home

Gene Babish is a 38-year-old single fellow who lives in a 10-foot × 12-foot (120-square-foot) tiny house in the backyard of the house of his sister Stephanie and brother-in-law Ronnie Coffey. Gene is a multitalented, can-do builder type of guy, including being a professional roofer. He helps with the Coffeys' excavating business, installing septic fields and preparing foundations. His passion is music. As his sister says, "He generally keeps to himself in good company."

Gene Babish

Here's Gene's story:

I love living in my little house. Life is great. It gives me a nice space of my own for when I need privacy. When I need a little quite time, I go out there. It is comfortable and it stays comfortable. It's mine. It also is a great space to bring my nephews out to and give them guitar lessons away from the rest of the family, so that others can do the things they might need to do. About 18 years ago I cut off two of my fingers on a conveyor and now I play my guitar the best that I can. I'm teaching my nephews to play. I really enjoy that.

My house has actually turned into a getaway space for other members of the family as well as myself. You might say at times that it is used more often than the main house. My brother-in-law, Ronnie, comes out and has a beer. My nephews, Peanut and Coltran, come out and listen to music, have snacks, and play the guitar with me. We can be laid back in my tiny home, in our own little world.

My nephews are actually jealous of me and the tiny house. They said they could have made it their club house. They got mad and went and bought themselves a tent, but they haven't used it yet. The tent just isn't the same as Uncle Gene's little house.

Before I came to live with my sister and Ronnie, I lived with my mom. She is divorced and I was taking care of her. Then my younger sister came to live with us. I decided it was time to find a new place. So I bought a tent and lived in it for almost a year before moving into my tiny house.

I have been married and divorced twice and have two children. I am living alone and guess I'm a bit of a natural loner. I just needed a small space that I could call home. I needed something affordable. Living in my tiny house is like I am 18 years old again. It's like I'm on my own little camping expedition, only better.

Gene Babish in front of his tiny home with the family dog Hogan. Gene's home is 120 square feet and is actually a detached bedroom from the main house. The house is totally insulated but not wired. You can see the outdoor extension cord that provides power from the main house. Gene's house is built on skids and can be easily moved with a tractor.

My sister, Stephanie, and brother-in-law, Ronnie, are nice enough to let me live on their property and to use their home facilities, such as the bath and kitchen. I use their electricity, hot water, washing machine, and dryer. In exchange I work around the house doing chores. I try to do the things I can to help out, like mowing and taking the kids for periods of time when it is helpful. I work with Ronnie in his excavating business full time.

If I was not living here in this tiny house, I would be living in that tent. The tent was nine feet × nine feet (81 square feet) and I moved it all over Rockbridge County. Sometimes I would stay in a campground. Sometimes my friends would invite me to their properties. Many times I would go to my friends' places and they would invite more people up and we would play music.

The inside of Gene's house has the warm glow of knotty-pine paneling. The open-beam ceiling makes the space seem bigger and more elegant. The wood also provides that fresh woody smell.

Before living in the tent, I was living in an apartment. I got tired of paying rent to live in a run-down place. The apartment was a three-bedroom, and for me it was just way too much space. Too much space to clean, too much space to fill, just too much. If I were to change anything in my tiny house, I would take one of the windows out and put a door in and expand out the back. I would add a little two-story with a loft. I actually think my tiny house would be perfect if it were on wheels so I could move it around.

Having my own tiny home in my sister's backyard has brought richness and meaning back into my life. It's brought us back together as a family. I so value the quality time I have with my nephews. Otherwise, I never would have known what a joy it is to be a contributing member of my family. Thank you Tiny House Company for making this possible.

— Gene Babish

My plans are to continue to work with the excavating business, and I might possibly go back to doing roofing. That is what I know and do best. I am happy here. I am safe, and I enjoy being with my nephews, playing with them and helping out. I will continue to live in my little house. It's my home.

The problem with Gene's situation is that the shed does not meet code if it were called a house. It was not an ideal situation but it worked to help him get his life together after some tough times.

The problem with housing seems to be getting greater. Chapter 12 on housing the unhoused discusses this nationwide problem.

Chapter 4:

Tiny Houses We Have Built

Tiny homes we have constructed come in a variety of shapes, sizes, and designs. Some look like fantasy retreats, others like lodges, and some like playhouses. Here are a few examples.

Andy's Weekender

This 24-foot × 12-foot (268-square-foot) tiny house was designed and built by Andy Lee. It is a full-feature cottage with

The Weekender is a full-featured tiny home with kitchen, bath, and sleeping loft. The tiny cottage includes an abundance of style with cedar siding and a cedar shake roof, handmade shutters and window boxes, and a stained-glass octagon window. Lots of windows and French doors allow much natural light.

a kitchen, bath, and sleeping loft. It has cedar siding, a cedar shake roof, handmade wood shutters and window boxes, and a custom octagon stained-glass window on the upper side.

In back, a double French door opens to the large deck that helps bring the outdoors inside. The deck becomes an outdoor dining room in good weather.

It is built to exceed code, with six-inch stud walls. This allows for super insulation and long-term energy savings.

This tiny house was placed on a flatbed truck and transported to a permanent foundation.

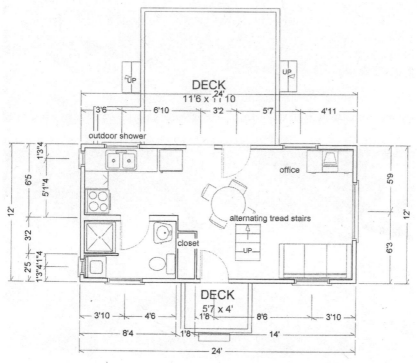

This is the floor plan of the Weekender tiny house. Full-featured kitchen (including dishwasher), bath and shower, room for a small dining table and foldout couch or built-in loft bed with a desk underneath. The bathroom includes space for an Equator clothes processor (a combination washer/dryer) beside the shower.

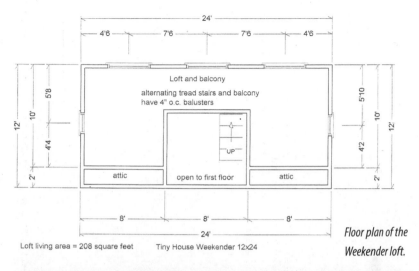

Loft and balcony

alternating tread stairs and balcony
have 4" o.c. balusters

UP

attic | open to first floor | attic

24'

4'6 — 7'6 — 7'6 — 4'6

12' 10' 5'8 4'4 2'

5'10 10' 4'2 2' 12'

8' — 8' — 8'

24'

Loft living area = 208 square feet   Tiny House Weekender 12x24

Floor plan of the Weekender loft.

Moving day for the Weekender. The porches were unbolted and set aside while the house was easily lifted by a crane and put on a flatbed truck to deliver. That's Andy guiding the house toward the truck. You must admit that this guy has leverage! Notice that the back side of the Weekender has dormer windows, Craftsman-style shaped rafter tails, and double French doors, which lead to the 12-foot × 12-foot cedar deck. We sold this house before finishing the decks.

Setting the tiny house on a very steep hillside. The crane had to work around the phone line and place the cottage on its foundation without bumping into trees.

More Room for Guests

Below is an example of a 12-foot × 20-foot (240-square-foot) cottage we built in Tryon, North Carolina, as a bed-and-breakfast expansion. It is a guest cabin. This little house has a kitchenette and three-quarter bath at one end. The sleeping/sitting area is at the other end, with a small dining area in the center. A ladder leads to the sleeping loft, which measures about three feet high, suitable only for storage or for a small child. This tiny house is in a forest about 20 yards behind the main house. The site contains mountain laurel and rhododendron bushes that the owner did not want us to disturb. Using any kind of

Nestled in the woods about 20 yards from the main house, this little cabin is designed to match the roof pitch, siding, and colors of the main house.

The inside of this tiny cottage is finished in tongue-and-groove knotty pine and tastefully furnished in a lake camp style. The bathroom is just to the left of the kitchen.

The photo above shows the loft above the kitchen. You can see the pull-down ladder for access. The fan provides whole-house ventilation. With the addition of a railing, this small loft could be used for sleeping for a small child or for storage.

backhoe or small dozer to dig a foundation was out of the question. Instead, we dug pier holes by hand with a post hole digger and mixed and poured the concrete footers by hand. We carried in all the lumber and building materials along a well-worn path.

The little cabin turned out better than any of us had hoped. The 12-foot × 10-foot deck (120 square feet) in front has built-in benches and flower boxes overlooking the wooded hillside and provides a wonderful place to sit and visit. The double kitchen window frames a beautiful view of the distant mountains as you sit with morning coffee and watch the sunrise. The roof pitch, color, and style match the larger main house up the hill. The inside is pine with custom matching cabinets.

Now, we often build tiny homes on trailers so they can be delivered to the site and set in place with a large crane.

Sun Block House

This 1,000-square-foot house is made of special Sparfil insulating concrete blocks and is situated for optimal passive solar gain in the winter. We are really excited about building with insulated concrete blocks because of their versatility. They are easy to work with and offer tremendous thermal advantages. However, we do not recommend their use for below-grade basements or foundations. Unfortunately, the Sparfil Company no longer makes their insulated concrete blocks for the American market.

Inside this solar home are hardwood floors throughout, with heating coils winding underneath the flooring for radiant heat. No cold feet in this house! The spacious wrap-around deck is a wonderful place for parties or to sit quietly watching the world go by. We placed deciduous shade trees along the south and west to help with summer cooling.

The red doors and other house features utilize feng shui — the Chinese art of energy flow. Note the adorable shed we built on the right, which follows the lines and pitch of the main house. This is insulated and could be used as an extra bedroom. It doesn't have electricity or plumbing, but they could be easily added.

We built this house using special insulated concrete blocks that were dry-stacked then finished inside and out with Fiberglass reinforced stucco.

Virginia Guest Cottage

This cottage was designed by the co-author, Andy Lee. It offers a very small footprint, measuring 18 feet × 18 feet. There are 324 square feet on the first floor and 150 square feet on the second floor for a total living space of 484 square feet. The 8-foot × 16-foot deck on the back of the house offers an excellent shaded area for outdoor living.

Tiny House Company built it for our clients in 2002 for about $35,000, not including land, well, or septic system. The house sits on a pier foundation with crawl space.

Downstairs there is room for a bath with shower, a kitchenette, a dining area in the extended bay window, and a living room. Under the stairs there is a closet for storage, and beneath the house is a fairly large crawl space for storage. There is also a storage closet under the eaves of the upstairs room.

The upstairs has room for a double bed on one side of the stairway, and a single bed on the other. A wall at the stairway provides a degree of privacy between the two bed areas. This upstairs could, in fact, be made into two rooms, although the smallest would measure only about 6 feet × 14 feet, probably only large enough for a small child.

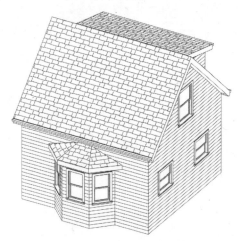

Nonetheless, a couple or a single parent with one child could live very comfortably in this house for an extended period of time.

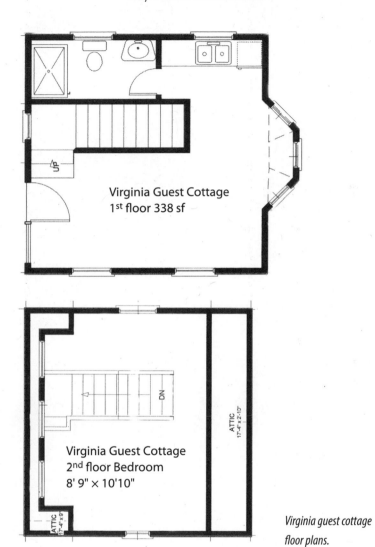

Virginia Guest Cottage
1st floor 338 sf

Virginia Guest Cottage
2nd floor Bedroom
8' 9" × 10'10"

ATTIC
17'-4" x 2'-10"

ATTIC
17'-4" x 8"

Virginia guest cottage
floor plans.

Chapter 5

Tiny Homes To Go

THROUGHOUT THE WORLD AND SINCE THE BEGINNING OF TIME people have moved with the seasons and taken their tiny homes with them. Examples are yurts, tents, lodges, domes, tipis, and Conestoga and gypsy wagons. For over a thousand years gypsy wagons and caravans have traveled across Europe and Britain.

We intuitively feel that there is a market niche for tiny homes on wheels. Even though tiny homes on wheels are movable, they are different from recreational vehicles (RVs) in that tiny homes are not intended to travel down highways at high speeds for extended periods. If you build your tiny home on a trailer you can move it from property to property occasionally and even across the country once or twice if necessary. Once you locate it on

Gypsy wagon.

the site where you choose to use your tiny home, you can either leave it on its trailer for easy moving in the future, or remove it from the trailer and set it on some form of foundation.

Designing and building a tiny house on a trailer differs in several ways from building one on a foundation. First, of course, you will have to consider transport restrictions and load limitations. For most federal and state highways, the combination of trailer and tiny house height can be no more than 13 feet 6 inches tall. If you are moving your home just a short distance and are sure the area is clear of overhead wires and tree branches, you can exceed this limit somewhat. For example, we recently moved one tiny house that was nearly 15 feet tall, but we didn't have to go under any bridges or electricity wires that were lower than that. The move was not legal in the strictest sense, but it was safe and well escorted and only a few miles on back roads, so we went ahead with it.

You also have to keep the overall width of your portable tiny house within the restrictions established by your state. For example, in Virginia any load over 10 feet wide and up to the 16-foot maximum width has to have an overwide load permit and be accompanied by an escort vehicle in the front and another in the rear. The measurement is taken at the widest part of the house, generally the eaves.

Length is not so critical for over-the-road transport, unless your destination is at the end of a twisted little path where a long vehicle will have trouble negotiating the curves. Many of the park-model tiny homes that we sell are 34 feet long with an attached 10-foot porch, making their overall length 44 feet. There are several modular home companies that can manufacture housing sections up to 66 feet long and transport them on specially built heavy-duty carriers.

Another consideration, if you are building your house on a trailer, is to make sure your plumbing, electrical, and HVAC installation can accommodate the trailer framing. We built one tiny house on a trailer where the toilet had to be moved two inches so the drain could fit inside the metal frame of the trailer.

You will also want to install some manner of waterproofing membrane on the underside so the floor insulation doesn't get wet if you move the trailer on a rainy day. We use heavy-duty plastic and staple it securely to the underside of the floor joists as we install the floor on the trailer. Also, you will want to have shutters over the windows or some other form of protection to keep the windowpanes intact during transport. Unlike a car windshield, which is tempered glass, typical house windows are fragile and very likely to crack if hit by road gravel.

We don't use Sheetrock inside a tiny house that is to be moved, because we are always concerned about cracks in the Sheetrock joints. Instead, we use either solid pine logs or one-inch × six-inch tongue-and-groove eastern white pine boards, which are very attractive and much more in keeping with the charm and style of tiny cottages that we build.

The overall weight of the house is also a consideration when designing and building one for portability. If you are using a lightweight utility trailer, you are limited to about 7,000 pounds of house weight, which is easy enough to achieve if you use light framing materials and finish materials and if your house size isn't much larger than, say, 10 feet × 20 feet. Stay away from extra-thick walls, heavy dimensional roof shingles, and drywall, all of which are heavy and can be replaced by much lighter materials such as 2 × 2 walls, metal roofing panels, and pine interior walls.

If you are planning to build the house and then move it only one time, you can hire someone with a heavy-duty trailer and truck to move the house. You can lift the house onto the trailer, and then lift it onto your new foundation with a hired crane.

If you have built your tiny house on a trailer but don't want to hire a crane, haul the tiny house to your destination, then use jacks to lift the house clear of the trailer. Remove the trailer, then install the permanent piers and lower the house onto them.

Lessons From the RV and Boating Industries

We can learn a tremendous amount about space utilization and comfort by studying both the recreational vehicle industry and the recreational boating industry. Boat builders, RV manufacturers, and marine design engineers have designed ways to conserve space, provide storage and utility, and equip their cabins with the latest in technology to convert what might otherwise be a cramped, restrictive, dysfunctional shoe box into a spacious, comfortable, efficient, and fun living environment.

In fact, the idea of little mobile homes with finely crafted living space isn't new at all. In his charming little book, *Free Wheeling Homes*, David Pearson takes us on a delightful tour through a history of colorful and functional gypsy wagons and caravans. Pearson has illustrated his book with dozens of beautiful color photographs of recreated and restored wagons and caravans. His book offers hundreds of ideas on how we can embellish our living spaces into art and make our surroundings fun, appealing, and satisfying.

Not only is mimicking the artistry of ancient gypsy wagons and modern recreational vehicles useful in our tiny house design process, we can also use miniaturized RV support systems such as water and sewer mechanics, heating and air conditioning equipment, electrical systems, and transport systems as models of how we can use less energy for better results. These are all things that can inform our design process and make our tiny houses more livable and infinitely more enjoyable.

We can also learn from the construction sequences used by the RV manufacturers. They build the recreational vehicles indoors at a series of work stations that make up an assembly line.

The unit moves from station to station, where trained opera-
tives perform tasks in sequence.

Much of the interior of the RV is actually finished before the
outside skin is applied, thus saving time and labor. Tasks can
be performed from outside the building in a standing position.

When we look at recreational vehicles and compare them to
tiny houses, it becomes clear that the one true way to make housing less expensive is to make it smaller. For example, in a typical
new home of today, the master bedroom might be as large as 400
square feet, compared to a comfortable but compact master bedroom in my travel trailer that is only 64 square feet, including
two shirt closets and a large storage compartment under the bed.

Nationally, there are nearly one million full-time and part-
time RV residents who are doing wonderfully well in homes that
are very much representative of the tiny house concept. Even
the largest recreational vehicles have less than 300 square feet
of living space. Many full-time RV folks are doing just fine in a
traveling home containing less square footage than their former
suburban living room. Probably two-thirds of the full-timers
travel from place to place, either following the sun or visiting
as much of our beautiful country as possible. Other full-time
RV residents park their travel trailer or motor home in a campground or on private land and live there full time, usually with
semi-permanent connections to water, sewer, and electricity.

Park Trailers

Park trailers are built on a trailer and towed to a permanent or
semipermanent site. These mobile tiny homes are legally classi-
fied under a category of recreational vehicle called "park trailer."
Park trailers have a wide range of possibilities for semipermanent and permanent housing. Legally, to be built on a trailer,
they can be no wider than 12 feet and no longer than 33 feet.
The overall size of the park trailer cannot exceed 400 square feet.

Because park trailers are built as recreational vehicles, it might be possible for you to park one on your land without a building permit. This is not guaranteed, because zoning laws vary tremendously in different localities. Check with your local zoning officials. But if you can park it under the RV code, this means you probably won't need a permit to park it and won't necessarily have to buy another building lot, which might be required with a permanent building.

Even though park trailers come under the recreational vehicle building guidelines, they are not meant to be towed day after day from site to site as is a travel trailer. They are just too bulky and not at all streamlined.

Financing is also available for the park models, and they can qualify under home equity loans as long as you own the land they will be sitting on. Check with your mortgage broker for plans and rates.

Park-model tiny homes built by Tiny House Company and our associates are either log cabin style, stick built, or built with structural insulated panels (SIPs). The SIPs and stick-built units give you the flexibility for the house to be finished to match the neighborhood where it will be parked or set. For example, if your main house has painted clapboard siding then you can use the same style and color clapboard siding, on the tiny house to match and blend in with the larger house.

Copper Top Cabin

We nicknamed one of the tiny homes we built on a trailer Copper Top. It has a copper roof, bay window, and white cedar exterior shingles. This little home is a real charmer! The bath has a shower, toilet, lavatory, and 12-gallon hot water heater. The kitchen has a stainless steel sink and Formica countertop, under-counter refrigerator, microwave oven, and built-in cabinets.

It has red oak flooring in the living room and kitchen and vinyl flooring in the bath.

The windows and door are Andersen Thermopane, with grills between the double panes. The walls, roof, and floors are insulated to R13. The interior is finished with knotty pine tongue-and-groove boards. The tiny cottage is fully wired and plumbed to code and is ready to connect to house power and water and sewer.

This shows the authors with Copper Top, and the Blue Ridge Parkway in the background. This photo opportunity was set up by Virginia Living *Magazine for an article on Tiny Homes. Copper Top is one of the custom, handcrafted, 10-foot × 22-foot (220-square-foot) ready-to-go on a trailer tiny homes built by Tiny House Company.*

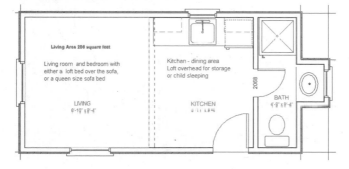

Floor plan of Copper Top Cabin. Note the design of the tiny, efficient, complete bath. The bay window that contains the lavatory also adds visual interest to the home's exterior design.

The kitchen inside Copper Top includes a microwave oven, refrigerator, and cabinet space. The three-piece bath is behind the door. A loft above the kitchen provides additional sleeping or storage space.

The bath is complete with toilet, sink, and shower and is equipped with attractive, quality fixtures. Though small, this bath is efficient, comfortable, and beautiful.

The interiors of many tiny cabins by Tiny House Company are finished with inviting knotty pine, and well-placed windows provide a naturally well-lit space and a visually appealing atmosphere. An octagon window above offers more light and natural ventilation and lends an artistic flair to the home's design.

New England Style Tiny House

We designed and built this 10-foot × 16-foot (160-square-foot) tiny home in a distinctively New England style. It has a cedar-shingle roof, octagon window, and exterior board-and-batten siding ready for any choice of colors. This home is an inviting, cozy cottage ready to please those who enter. The bath has a shower and toilet and 12-gallon hot water heater. The kitchen has a single-bowl stainless steel sink and Formica countertop, under-counter refrigerator, microwave oven, and maple cabinets.

There is a tiny loft that can be used as a sleeping loft for a child or for storage. The flooring in the living room and kitchen is red oak, with vinyl flooring in the bath. The windows and exterior door are energy efficient, and the walls, roof, and floors

This 160-square-foot New England style tiny cottage by Tiny House Company is handcrafted and built on a trailer for easy relocation. This cottage is especially suitable for a studio, home office, or weekend getaway. This particular tiny house belongs to Ray Pealer, who is featured in Chapter Three.

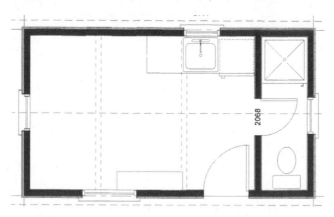

Floor plan of the Tiny New England Cottage. Dimensions of this cottage are 10 feet × 16 feet. The interior of this home feels spacious, as well-placed windows and the French door add natural light and a sense of openness.

are insulated to R13. The interior is finished with tongue-and-groove eastern white pine. The cottage is fully wired and plumbed and ready to connect to house power and water and sewer.

The trailer that the little house sits on can be licensed for over-the-road transport. It has two 3,500 pound axles with brakes on one axle. It has a 2⅝" trailer ball and a mechanical tongue jack. For short distances the trailer can be towed with a half-ton pickup with a Class III weight-distributing hitch or with a heavy-duty pickup truck with Class III hitch. However, if you are planning on towing the trailer at highway speeds for an extended period you will probably want to hire a trucker who has at least a one-ton tow vehicle.

Small Log Cabin Homes

These 12-foot × 33-foot (396-square-feet) log cabins come complete and ready to occupy. All you have to do is connect

One of our favorites. This log cabin has a dormer that adds light and more spaciousness inside. The optional dormer costs only $1,250. This cabin is on a permanent foundation, with the rear deck added to extend the end deck for a wrap-around porch.

These two cabins show the covered porch with a sliding six-foot door (above) and a single door below. Note how the different finishes on the porches give an individual touch. Both these cabins are still on their trailers. The stairs and side deck can be removed by unbolting them from the house. Note the brick skirt (below), which can also be done with rock or cultured stone, or you can use lattice panels to enclose the bottom of the trailer (above).

to water, sewer, electricity, and propane. We have three models. Some folks want to add porches, which can be done at the factory and included in the base price, or the porch can be added on site by a local contractor after the cabin is situated.

This shows two cabins with a ten-foot covered porch and set on permanent stone foundations. The stairs and side decks are added on site.

This cabin is still on its trailer but has a full deck across the front. Decks can be bolted to the house and removed if needed before moving.

This cabin shows how a roof-extended country porch can be added for that sit-on-the-porch-and-chat-a-while look. This particular cabin is on a permanent foundation.

Note that all our log cabins have metal roofs that help with fire protection. Metal roofs are also better suited for rainwater harvesting than some other roofing material choices. As Joe and Krysti Hamlin, our builders in Campobello, South Carolina, state, "Our mix of modern methods and traditional craftsmanship create the most durable and attractive cabins available. Each cabin we build is one both you and we can be proud of."

Tumbleweed Tiny Homes

A good friend of ours, Jay Shafer, is also a tiny house enthusiast and builder. Jay walks his talk. He designs, builds, and lives in a house smaller than some people's bathrooms. He calls his tiny home Tumbleweed.

Jay's decision to live in 130 square feet arose, in part, from some concerns he has about the impact a larger house has on the environment. Added to that, Jay does not have a desire to pay for and maintain more space than he feels he needs to be happy.

Jay is a pioneer in the tiny home movement. His home has appeared in several magazines. He constantly gets letters with questions about how to build and live in tiny homes. People love to share stories with Jay of the little places they have encountered and inhabited.

Jay's tiny house is mounted on a conventional four-ton equipment trailer for easy portability behind a typical heavy-duty pickup truck. Inside the tiny home he has room for a small woodstove, a gravity-fed shower and sink, a composting toilet, and a tiny cookstove. The photovoltaic

> My Tumbleweed tiny home meets my needs without exceeding them. The simple, slower lifestyle my home affords is a luxury for which I am supremely grateful.
>
> — Jay Shafer

Jay Shafer's Tumbleweed Tiny Home. Note the inviting porch to sit a spell and the Gothic window that gives his tumbleweed home that special look.

electric system provides power for the lights, fan, a stereo, and a tiny television. According to Jay's accounting of the construction costs, he has spent over $42,000 building this first prototype, which displays a very high level of materials and finish work.

Jay is constantly designing and refining his tiny home plans. The size of these houses ranges from 50 to 500 square feet. Their particular function will vary depending on the immediacy of their occupants' needs. What some would use as an office in the back yard another couple might choose to inhabit as a full-time residence.

> Be it a trailer, tree house, playhouse, or cabin, it seems that nearly everyone has an appreciation for some small place or another.
>
> — Jay Shafer

Every structure in Jay's portfolio is designed to accommodate year-round occupancy in any climate. Unlike most conventional travel trailers, RVs, and many cabins, each of the homes Jay illustrates is fully heated, insulated, and vented. Every unit makes the most of its small size by minimizing transitional areas like hallways and stairwells, maximizing storage space, and maintaining a simple exterior without unnecessary projections. Such uncomplicated exteriors reduce the amount of exposed surface area on each house to cut heating, cooling, and construction costs.

These little houses were created by using many of the same geometric principles traditionally used to proportion cathedrals. Old vernacular structures in the U.S. and Europe have provided further inspiration. The simple, formal designs that have resulted offer an excellent way to arrange most any space and make it beautiful.

In conclusion, we believe there is a housing niche for tiny homes on wheels. These mobile small homes usually are handcrafted and are constructed with heavier materials than an RV. They are not meant for long-distance travel but can be moved from place to place. We think of them as semi-permanent.

Chapter 6

Expanding A Tiny Home with Do-It-Yourself Construction

THERE ARE TIMES WHEN A LARGER HOME is needed and expansion is necessary. There are also times when it is necessary or desirable to do the work yourself. Over the years we have encountered many folks who are interested in building their own tiny home or expanding an existing smaller home. We have included the home renovation story of Tiny House Company's office manager Jennifer Bodnar to illustrate the challenges and rewards of home remodeling. Her experience and lessons learned might provide some valuable guidelines and insights to your own project.

Here is Jennifer's story.

＊＊＊＊＊

My husband Rick and I decided to transform our older home in beautiful Lexington, Virginia, into a living environment more suited to our lifestyle. We needed space. Rick has three teenage daughters. Everyone prefers their own room.

Life would be easier with a second bathroom, a bigger kitchen, storage space, and a separate master bedroom. Rick works at home most of the time and could be better organized with a home office instead of a corner.

Rick and Jennifer Bodnar.

My three stepdaughters, Martha, Claire, and Rebecca, are teaching me much about life and that sometimes the house can wait. While they are part of the inspiration for an expanded house, they are also often the inspiration for a much-needed break.

In addition to all these wants, the home is old, and the electrical, plumbing, and heating systems need updating, and the whole house needs to be insulated to meet the new model energy code.

In the beginning we thought about selling our little house and buying something more aligned to our wishes. Yet, after evaluating what is important to us in a house and location, as well as evaluating our alternatives in the local real estate market, it became clear that in order to achieve our ideal home we should stay put and transform our space.

Our idea of expansion started because we wanted more space to comfortably live as a family. But it grew to involve many design features that we really prefer. We determined that the critical element to gaining it all and staying within our budget was to do the work ourselves. We were inspired by visions of beauty, creativity, and finally having the space we need for our family and home offices.

Now two years into the renovation, I'd have to say there is much more than just the hammers and nails of the project to consider before diving into your own do-it-yourself home improvement. It is a dance of tasks, triumphs, and tribulations. While life is hectic and unorganized, it is really good. I feel fortunate, accomplished, and proud.

This is the story of our journey to a better home and an enhanced lifestyle. Included are a few tips to help you survive gracefully should you find yourself amidst your own do-it-yourself construction.

The Bodnars' 1,600-square-foot, 1920s home was renovated and expanded with a tiny house in back. The front steps and porch were condemned by the postal service, so that became one of the home's first renovation projects.

The Transformation

Throughout renovations we have had many realizations, including the necessity to keep our plan flexible to adapt to our changing needs over the three-year construction time. There is no plan truly set in stone until it is actually complete. Here is the overview of what we did and ended up with.

Our home's original footprint is two-story 25 feet × 36 feet (900 square feet per level, or 1,800 square feet total). There is a 25-foot × 28-foot detached cinder block garage located behind the house. With three bedrooms and one bath, our little abode was not necessarily a tiny home to begin with, but the original floor plan simply did not work for our family size and work-at-home lifestyle. The new addition and remodeling created interesting spaces designed to fit the flow of our lives perfectly.

We have a new layout for much of the original home. The kitchen and dining areas, once small and divided, are being expanded and combined into one larger, open space with a laundry room.

We built a connecting structure from the original house to the original garage. This is now a home office and rear entry and has a bathroom for clients. The kitchen, office, and master bedroom open onto the new courtyard, which is ideally situated for outdoor socializing.

This shows the courtyard in early stages, connecting the main house to the garage. The gable roof in the connecting addition was constructed to create consistency with the roofline on the front of the house as well as add visual interest to the courtyard space.

The once ugly, misused, and weathered cinder block garage was doing nothing for us but sheltering junk. We decided to make the garage into our master bedroom suite. We will finally have our privacy, and the three girls will get the upstairs of the house, where each can have her own room and a shared bath.

In order to transform the garage appropriately to suit our home's style and our preferences, we jacked up the roof of the garage and took out the cinder block walls, replacing them with 2 × 6 stud-framed walls so we could add insulation, and installed siding that matches the house.

Before we began construction, we needed to create enough storage space to shelter things that we didn't want to get rid of. It was critical to our home improvement project to have a space to store our overflow of home furnishings and to keep tools and materials out of the weather and safe from pilferage. Our solution was to build a nice little storage shed in the backyard.

The former cinder block garage is now the master bedroom suite. The room to the far right sits on the old garage foundation. On the left is the connecting addition that houses the home office, bath, and rear entry. The addition design provides a courtyard space with fireplace for outdoor socializing. The rear of the home will include a back deck for private lounging from the master bedroom suite.

The 8-foot × 12-foot shed in the backyard behind the new parking area holds the overflow of household items and tools during construction. It will be our new garden shed when the home construction is complete.

Things to Consider

We have taken on quite an ambitious remodeling project. Here are some steps that we went through in evolving our design and construction process. Hopefully, you can gather some ideas on how to make your project go smoothly and successfully.

Even though we did a tremendous amount of questioning and planning over a period of several months, there are still times that I wonder if we truly gave it enough thought. Our initial planning involved how much money we wanted to spend and what the design would be like. I can see now that we didn't spend enough time talking about the emotional and physical stress that we would place ourselves under while living in construction. I have grown to realize that do-it-yourself home remodeling is not a project, it is a lifestyle.

We began our home reconstruction as a newlywed couple of one year. In hindsight, the stress was more than I thought. We had to cope with the merging of families, living in a new city, being away from our extended families and friends, beginning new jobs, and learning our way as a new couple. A logical person would question whether taking on a major reconstruction project was a good idea. But we began to dream, and the dream soon took hold, and we were off on our home-improvement journey.

We are now moving into our third year of construction. I spend a lot of time thinking about the house design and how it will serve the design of our life. I suppose this deepening thought is in part because I have grown to believe that a do-it-yourself home-improvement project of substantial size becomes a being of its own, and this creation takes a part of you.

Lots of love, time, energy, and frustration can be funneled into this home. Do-it-yourself home construction is not a project, it is a lifestyle — at least on the scale on which we are involved.

I have grown to realize that do-it-yourself home remodeling is not a project, it is a lifestyle.

Before beginning any major home improvements, here are some questions you might ask yourself and think deeply on:

- *Am I ready for it physically, emotionally, and technically?*
- *Is this really where I want to spend my money and my time?*
- *What will I have to sacrifice in order to have this home expansion?*
- *What do I want most?*
- *Am I secure in what I want in my life in addition to wanting a larger home?*
- *Will I be ready to leave it behind when it is time?*
- *Am I sure I really want or need a larger home?*

As with many other choices in life, there is a possibility of getting in a bind and limiting your life's other possibilities. It may even cause considerable strain physically, emotionally, and financially if you try to juggle it all at once.

You're involved in a project that waits solely on you, or the two of you. It's there when you are tired, when you are stressed, when you don't have time, when you do have time but don't want to work on it, when it's cold, when it's hot, when it's not what you want to be doing. It's your project, and your responsibility.

Ultimately it's about how badly you really want a remodeled home or an addition to your house and how much you really want to do yourself.

It is also about how you and your partner will work together. Think of how your partner works and his or her personality. Think of how the two of you work together on other projects. It may give you an indication of what you can expect when working together in construction.

You should also consider the other stresses weighing on your life. Construction projects have resulted in a large number of divorces. You know your life, and you know your partner. So you can make an educated decision.

It is also important that you realize there are some real advantages to doing construction on your home yourself. Here are a few advantages you should consider.

Advantages of Do-It-Yourself

Flexibility. *The ability to change: change the design plan; change the schedule; change your mind. Flexibility is the utmost advantage of doing it yourself.*

Quality Supervision and Satisfying Outcome. *You may not be a professional, but no one can do it like you — to your standards, to your visions, to your comfort. If you do something and don't like it, you can easily tell yourself to redo it, or at least fine-tune it.*

No One Else to Deal With. *Doing it yourself doesn't have the infringement and fallout of having someone else in your home and someone else to address.*

Sometimes Less Money Spent. *To do a job yourself generally means saving money by not paying someone else to do the labor. However, doing the job poorly and having to redo gets costly.*

Your Creation and Your Accomplishment. *One of the greatest joys about doing it yourself is that the outcome is totally your creation. It has you in it. By doing it yourself you can enjoy a well-deserved sense of accomplishment!*

After you've considered all the above, if your decision is not to proceed, you have probably made a wise choice.

If your decision is to move forward and you are certain your changes will render a more functional lifestyle, then you are setting sail on an exciting journey that can bring you a lot of fulfillment.

Deciding On, Drawing, and Permitting Your Plans

Once Upon a Plan

Deciding upon and designing a plan is both a strong beginning and an ongoing process toward your better home. We spend hours and hours together dreaming of our home's transformation. Thinking of how we can restructure our home, both from a functional and design standpoint, absorbs much of our focus.

Before and during construction we have changed our minds and plans many times. It has caused more than a little doing, undoing, and redoing, but we are sure the changes are valid and valuable. We saved all of our drawings, and many times we look back and realize how our plans have evolved to a more suitable design for our needs.

We also know that we could not have changed our design so extensively if we had hired a contractor to do the work. The job may have been done more quickly, but it would not have been our best design. We would not have had nearly as much time to think about what we truly want or need. The more thought we have put into it, the better our plan has become.

So, how do you decide on a plan? Start with a lot of thought and sketching and asking yourself a lot of questions. Take inventory of your home's current design and what it offers you in functionality and space. What is wrong with it? How could it be better? What are you hoping to achieve with your remodel or addition? What will make your life simpler, more efficient, more exciting, and generally better suited to you?

When designing your plan, keep in mind that additions to your home should complement its existing style. The point is for it to be your style but to also blend with your existing home design. You may also want to ensure that your new home addition is in keeping with the theme and presence of the homes around it. For example, you may favor a new modernist or contemporary design, but it would look and feel out of place on a street lined with Craftsman bungalows.

There are great books available on the subject of merging your home's addition with your existing home design. One book that I enjoy reading is Adding To A House: Planning, Design, & Construction *by Philip S. Wenz. He explains that continuity with the shape, style, and spirit of the existing house is the key to successful addition design.*

Drawing and Redrawing Your Plans

After deciding on a plan, you will need to draw it. There are books available on drawing plans, such as Draw Your Own House Plans *by Mike and Ruth Wolverton.*

A better option is to purchase a low-cost, user-friendly architectural drawing program. The one that seems to be the most popular and able to turn out acceptable building plans with the least amount of learning curve is 3D Home Architect. You may choose to hire an architect or draftsperson to draw your plans. They can use your sketches and descriptions to fashion the design you want and need.

Permitting Your Plans — Hopefully Only Once

After drawing your plans, take them to your local building inspector to get a building permit. If you have questions regarding the requirements for a building permit, call your local building inspection department and ask what they need on the application. In some cases, they will only ask for a sketch of the floor plan, but they may also want plan views of how the house will look after the addition is built. These are called elevations. The building department will also want a sketch of the foundation or piers you plan under your addition.

The cost of a building permit is based on a percentage of your estimated home improvement cost. So you need a budget to show the building department. They will also want to know about how much time you think the remodeling will take. In our town the building permit is issued for two years. If your project takes longer you have to renew your permit.

Preparing a Budget and Schedule

Money

Preparing a budget and sticking to it takes some real self-discipline. Sometimes costs escalate because of the cost of building materials or subcontractors; other times the costs can get out of hand when you start adding things as the project progresses.

Creating a budget for the do-it-yourselfer involves research on product costs. Make a list before venturing out to the home improvement store. Then research the products at stores like Lowe's and Home Depot, or at specialty stores, and jot down the prices of the products that best fit your wants and needs. If you have a computer you will be able to locate many of your building supply costs from manufacturers' websites and from discussion boards. One place to check for costs is to join the discussion group at FineHomebuilding.com.

There are books for helping to estimate a home improvement project's cost, such as Exterior Home Improvement Costs, The Practical Guide for Homeowners and Contractors, and the companion Interior Home Improvement Costs, published by RS Means Company. They list materials, levels of difficulty, what to watch out for, and estimated material and contractor costs for a number of home remodeling projects and additions. They are available at Lowe's and Home Depot as well as Amazon.com.

It is important that your budget be relatively accurate. It is also important to include a large "fudge" factor for flexibility. Figure your budget on the high end instead of on the low end of the possibilities. This allows for unexpected price increases, materials forgotten, and, most of all, peace of mind when costs aren't exactly running on budget.

*How important it is to stick to your budget depends on your finan-
cial situation and how long you want to pay for the project. If you are at
risk of running out of money before the project is complete, then it is very
important that you have a realistic budget and do what it takes to stay
within the limits.*

Time

*Time seems to be never fully in your control. Don't think that you will al-
ways be running on schedule when it comes to construction. You will get
behind, and occasionally you will get ahead.*

*There will be things that will come up along the way that you just
could not have known about before beginning the project, especially
when it comes to remodeling older homes. There are often delays from
weather, waiting for inspectors, waiting for subcontractors or materials
and a host of other problems that can crop up unexpectedly. It's best just
to plan on delays from the beginning rather than get your hopes too high
on an unrealistic completion date.*

*If you are having trouble knowing just how long a project should
take, you might ask contractors in the area, your local building inspector,
or anyone who might be knowledgeable in construction.*

*The interior and exterior remodeling books I mentioned sometimes
show estimated completion times for various tasks. Keep in mind that the
times listed are for experienced workers, not the untrained do-it-yourselfer.
Set a schedule, but be versatile. Your sanity and motivation will demand it.*

Learning How to Do-It-Yourself

*There are two parts to learning how to do something on your own. First is
the physical challenge of doing it yourself, and then there is the emotional challenge. Construction can be overwhelming and yet so exciting. In
my experience, excitement turns to overwhelming and back again, and
the cycle just continues.*

*I feel the most excitement in the dreaming of what it will be like when
it is complete. I feel the most overwhelmed when I really want to be doing something else, anything else, but realize that I will never achieve the*

completed dream unless I do the work. Sometimes it's great. Sometimes it's hard. And sometimes everyone around me seems to be tired and frustrated with the project. It is easy to get frustrated when trying to do things that are new and doing so with limited knowledge.

One of the best ways of reducing do-it-yourself-related stress and frustration is to know as much as possible before you start. Break the construction down into smaller projects. When we don't know how to do something, we buy a book or a tape and learn, or we visit websites that might offer helpful information. You can gather useful information at hgtv.com or thisoldhouse.com. I also have learned many wonderful ideas and tips from watching Home & Garden television (HGTV).

A quote my high school English teacher posted in her classroom comes to mind: "If you fail to prepare, then you prepare to fail." Preparing ahead by reading how-to manuals, watching videos or home improvement shows, and reading instructions will save you a lot of suffering and time and money wasted.

You can be certain there is a book or video to help you with the job du jour. There are many excellent books listed in the Bibliography and References section of this book.

Another beneficial learning resource is your local building inspector. Our local inspector has become an invaluable source of information. Any time we have questions concerning what and when certain items should be inspected, we call the inspector. He also can tell us what our local building codes require.

In addition to consulting how-to construction manuals and knowledgeable individuals, take time to learn about tools. Having the right tools is key to building intelligently, efficiently, and beautifully. The correct tools help to make the large task of our addition possible. Our best advice is don't even try to do it without the right tools. You may incur some additional costs, but they will save you much time and difficulty and will help render a better finished product.

Over time we have gathered the knowledge of the right tools for a job. It is now clear that we could have produced a much better product *in many of our early projects had we only had the correct equipment at hand. You can either buy or rent, but make sure you have the right tool for the job every time.*

For example, I highly recommend a nail gun for framing and for finish work. Both Rick and I are inexperienced carpenters, and nailing boards together accurately and quickly was a problem for us until we bought the Paslode cordless nail gun. A $400 nail gun is expensive, but it will save frustrating thumb banging and nail bending and shave many hours off the job. At the end of the job we can sell the nail gun for at least half what we paid for it or simply keep it and be ready for future projects.

Rick's advice is to never buy a tool without a case if there's an option. If there's no option, maybe buy a toolbox and dedicate it as the home of the specific tool. We place each tool in its respective case along with related wrenches, oil, and replacement parts. When we need that tool it is right there on the shelf ready to go. Organization of tools is an important element if you are going to work efficiently. Tool organization will also help to reduce frustration and stress in your construction environment.

The best advice of all is the number one rule of construction: measure twice, cut once.

Living and Surviving in Construction

Living in construction requires a remarkably flexible attitude. You may find yourself living in a half-finished project for months or years longer than you originally planned. It took us five years to fully complete our ideal home. That is, if one can say their home is ever truly complete. I must tell you that living in construction is hard. That is the bottom line, but for us it was worth it and we have the home of our dreams.

In order to deal with the frustration of living in construction, I believe one must allow oneself to be inspired. Take time to dream. Take time to do the things that you really enjoy, especially during the periods of the project that you truly do not enjoy. I believe that staying inspired is key. Pinpoint what it is that you enjoy about the project and your home, and find the time to do it.

Work one less hour on roofing and use that hour to work on your land-scaping, for example. Work on another portion of the project that excites you, as long as it is a project that is productive to the overall completion and not a project that will later get destroyed by further construction. Do whatever it is that keeps you excited about your home improvement. Also, take time to go off on a tangent and do something totally differ-ent. Some weekends we totally leave the project behind. There has to be a balance between doing what you enjoy and doing the things you don't if you are going to survive the process happily.

The dream is what carries me through the dust and debris. When the walls are crumbling around me, I remember my dream, and it's all worth it — stress included.

— Jennifer Bodnar

Cleaned up for this photo opportunity, the kitchen and dining areas are examples of the uprooted, dysfunctional, messy living-in-construction lifestyle. Too little space for too many things. Kitchen cabinets supported by barstools, washer and dryer temporarily positioned in the refrigerator and pantry space. Unfinished plywood floors, with seams that trap dirt. Yet the open stud walls give that airy, open floor plan feeling!

There's a whole new set of rules when you're living in construction. And it can drive you crazy if you don't change your way of thinking. Relax. Let go of normal structure. Realize that things will once again be as they were, only better with your new, more functional home. But realize that for now your world is altered. Do your best to relax within a setting that is anything but restful.

The Dangers of Construction

We have had some mishaps: falling through the floor joists, skinned chin, scraped legs, twisted ankle, cut fingers, allergy episodes, splinters, hammer falling off ladder onto nose (those holes in the tops of step ladders are there for a reason). Without a doubt, we have been very lucky, as our injuries have been minor in comparison to the possibilities.

Being safe truly overrides everything else in the construction process. If you make a mistake, so what — it costs you time, money, and energy, but do you still have all your fingers, toes, and nose? Then so what, you made a mistake, that's all.

Common Sense Safety

Tips Learned the Hard Way...

- *Don't climb on an unstable ladder. Don't set a ladder on any material that may slip or allow the ladder to slip. Don't climb a ladder or work on a roof in shoes that have soles with no grip.*
- *Don't work in an elevated situation when your shoes or the surface you are climbing on is slick, or even if you believe they may be slick.*
- *Don't reach beyond your comfortable distance to work, especially while on a ladder. Take the time to move the ladder to where it needs to be instead of overextending yourself and inviting a possible disaster.*
- *Don't leave tools on the top of your stepladder. You will very probably forget they are there, and the next time you move the ladder they will fall on you.*
- *Try to avoid working from ladders when you are alone. Things do sometimes happen, even when doing your best to take precautions.*

- *Don't walk on open floor joists or rafters. Take the time to put down a piece of plywood to provide a work platform.*
- *Don't lift things that are too heavy for you. Ask for help. Hire help when needed.*
- *Don't stand in the direct path of a nail from a nail gun. There are times when you will find yourself in the very near vicinity of the nail, for instance if you are on one side of a board and the nail gun operator is on the other, nailing in your direction.*
- *Be aware of your surroundings.*
- *Wear safety goggles when cutting materials and when using power tools, especially nail and staple guns. In some situations, wear safety goggles when working above your head. In general, wear safety goggles as often as possible.*
- *Listen to yourself and your feelings about the job situation. If you feel unusually uncomfortable, insecure, or nervous about a particular situation, for instance, being on a roof or doing electrical work, then do all things possible to make yourself secure. At times, the better part of valor is to hire a professional to take care of tasks that make you nervous.*

There are some projects that it's best to contract out. We hired a contractor to pour the foundation, a plumber who allowed Rick to assist in the plumbing, and an electrician to make the connection of our new circuits to the existing electrical panel. Other than that it's all us.

I am deeply enjoying our home construction project. I get a genuine sense of excitement, contentment, and fulfillment. It adds to my life as well as my home. Even with the stress included, it is an elevating experience. I would not choose our path differently.

I appreciate and enjoy working with Patricia and Andy and the many subcontractors at Tiny House Company. Their homes and ideas are fantastic and inspiring. While in the middle of expansion, I really believe in the tiny house movement. Small spaces can be exciting, comforting, fitting, and freeing. I think often of living in less space and having more time, freedom, and money because of its efficiency.

Rick and I both wish you all the best as you begin to design and develop your home remodeling project.

The construction took five years, and we have created a more functional and comfortable abode. The home is us, not because we live in it but because we created it. Our feelings of accomplishment and excitement are fantastic!

Chapter 7:

Clutter Control and Stuffology

Definition of Stuff:

Stuff (*stuf*) *n*. Informal. 1. Household or personal articles collectively: belongings. 2. Worthless objects; refuse or junk. 3. Slang. To pack tightly, fill up; cram. Often used derogatorily: *His head is stuffed with silly notions. I'm stuffed* (overate, glutton). From old French *estoffe*, provisions, from *estoffer*, to cram, Late Latin *stuppare*, to plug up from Latin *stuppa*, plug, cork.

Stuffology (*stuf-oleje*) *n*. 1. The study of stuff.

STUFFOLOGY IS ONE OF THOSE EMERGING WORDS in the English language. I first heard it used by Carolyn Myss in her talk about "Spiritual Madness." Carolyn was using stuffology in the context of personal issues, as in "dealing with one's stuff."

Looking at my life and ongoing transformations, I realize that my *stuff*, in all its permutations and at all levels, is an extension of myself. This includes not just things but also beliefs, thought patterns, habits, groups, personal history issues. Things, feelings, and stuff I own are there because I used my energy, skills, money, and intention to bring them into my life. That includes people.

> The world is too much with us; late and soon, getting and spending, we lay waste our powers: little we see in Nature that is ours.
>
> — William Wordsworth

In really looking at all my stuff accumulation through my various life phases, interests, and businesses, I realize just how much of it I don't use or even want any more.

Everyone goes through phases. Likes and dislikes change with the decades. If only my tastes hadn't changed so widely, I could have saved tens of thousands of dollars. But that is what the fashion designers and consumer society literally bank on.

Once I recognized the extent of my personal overload of obsolete (to me) stuff, I began to systematically eliminate things from my living spaces. I began by finding new homes for things that my changing taste and current aesthetics had made obsolete for my needs, yet had intrinsic value someone else would appreciate.

Clutter can be particularly annoying in a tiny house. When you don't have a lot of room to begin with, it is imperative that you use your space thoughtfully.

I also sorted through redundant items such as two lawn mowers and three vacuum cleaners. At first, some things were hard to let go of. For example my patinaed "early-student era" sofa that was so comfortable but worn beyond rehabilitation. Neither Goodwill nor Habitat would take it. That couch held a lot of dear memories for me, but it was time to let it go. I even teared up a bit at the dumpster as it tumbled in.

As I decluttered and destuffed, I came to the realization that I had far more living space just because of less stuff. Feeling very encouraged by my newfound space, I kept dejunking, sorting, organizing, and clearing out stuff that didn't serve me. This included things, beliefs, mental patterns, and even body fat. Yes, I had even stuffed myself and was about 50 pounds overweight. I viewed my excess fat as body clutter that had to go, never to return again!

For releasing things, I made it a game to find useful and appropriate homes for them. For example, government surplus filing cabinets that I had acquired over 30 years ago, along with sagging book shelves and older office materials, I gave to

Goodwill so that they might be used by an entrepreneur just starting up their new business.

From the corporate viewpoint, when Good Earth Publications gets book orders from prison inmates or nonprofit institutions, we include bonus books along with their regular book order. This helps decrease our outdated stock and overflowing office library.

Clothes, linens, shoes, and other odd items I offered to friends and those I knew who could benefit from them. eBay, craigslist, and local bulletin boards became a wonderful way to find new and profitable homes for stuff.

In my office I took the same approach for dealing with clutter. I made it a habit to handle each paper only once. Before, I would let a month's worth of mail stack up before sorting it. Sometimes a stack might get shuffled into another paper pile and disappear until some critical time when I realized a bill was overdue but I hadn't seen the invoice because I never opened the envelope! That would lead to a frantic search. Now I triage the mail daily, sorting it into action and bills, filing and recycling.

I put the bills/action in a wall holder on my office wall so they won't get lost. Any papers I want to keep for later reading I put in my reading inbox. Articles or items of interest I file. I use printed labels because my handwriting is so bad.

Over several months of my stuffology efforts, I found that house cleaning became easier. Not just a little easier — it was a lot easier. Cleaning almost stopped being a chore.

Now I can find things faster because of having to search through less clutter. Have you ever had something in your hand and set it down for just a second while you answered the phone, and then couldn't find it again? Before, I always blamed gremlins. Now, the gremlins seem to have evaporated. There are simply fewer places for things to hide, thanks to my reorganization efforts.

A true feeling of freedom and relief emerged that I found surprising. I also gained a deep sense of satisfaction of having just enough. I had organization and control where before was clutter and dust-covered chaos. I was a phoenix rising out of my own debris.

It's interesting how the universe can communicate. While working on this chapter, my Yogi tea fortune was the message "True wealth is the ability to let go of your possessions."

I meditated on this proverb. It's true that the less I own the more I have. This sounds like a paradox but it isn't. I now have less stuff but take more joy from my fewer possessions. I have more shelf space, more closet room, more file space, more time free from searching for things. I have gained more simplicity. But the best part is that I have freedom from wanting more; I am content. That's something you can't buy. The Tao Te Ching, the ancient book of wisdom phrased it as "Those who know they have enough are rich."

Letting go of so many possessions does not mean I'm poor. *Au contraire!* Through my investments, businesses, royalties, attitude, and continuing education I am very well off. But the truth is that my wealth is not in finances or things.

My authentic wealth comes from staying in my integrity and purposeful work that contributes to possibly making this a better world. My riches come from having a purposeful life. I endow myself with learning and being the best I can be given whatever condition I'm in or facing. I love to study and have had multiple careers in my life. One of my personal mottoes is "Retire early and often; recreate myself."

My true fortune lies in my ability to love, to be grateful, and be of compassionate service to the world. My greatest reward is peace of mind and knowing that I can handle whatever comes my way. Some people think I'm unreasonably happy. I believe that is one of the most desirable ways to be. How could one be richer than to be happy most of the time? Prosperity is a conscious state of mind; it is not only about money.

Redundancy Causes Chaos

Let's talk about having multiples of one item so that one will always be available when needed. For example, I like a certain type of mechanical pencil. So I bought six of them. It didn't work. When I had only one I could find it. When I had six I couldn't find any.

So decreasing the redundancy of things has helped me be organized and has been a timesaver as I don't have to search through as much clutter to find the item I want. This redundancy reduction includes dishes, tools, hats, clothes, boxes, books, pans, cookware, and even pet food bowls.

Many people who are attracted to the tiny house concept might be seeking simpler lives through such conscious living choices as downsizing and living with lower monthly expenses so they don't have to work so much.

There is a worldwide grassroots movement spawned by such books as *Your Money or Your Life* by Vicki Robin and Joe Dominguez, which asks the question, "How much is enough?"

Folks who are following this trend tend to value their free time, which often means getting by with part-time jobs or living off investments. Living simpler and freer.

> Clutter control is as much about organization as it is about having your possessions available to serve you when you need it.

As a current tiny house inhabitant, I love my creature comforts and am not about to give up any of my stuff-treasures. Personal treasures don't necessarily translate to clutter. For example, I have African masks and Tibetan art collections from my many years of working overseas. There is more art than wall space. So I rotate my art. I have also given some of it away and donated a few of the finer pieces to museums so that others can appreciate them.

Stuffology can be a hot topic. I have had people angrily tell me how they have worked hard for their treasures. They are not about to give stuff up. I just smile and reaffirm their feelings. I try and put them at ease by saying that your personal stuff is exactly that — your private, personal stuff. Stuff makes your home unique and expresses your individual personality. Keep the stuff you want; tithe or get rid of stuff if it no longer serves you.

If downsizing seems daunting, keep in mind how encumbering is it to work just to pay for heated and air-conditioned housing and storage for your stuff. Then the stuff owns you and not the other way around. All that stuff has no feelings about you or your well-being.

Renting self-storage units has become increasingly popular. Most folks would rather rent a storage bin for $50 or more per month ($600 per year) than to sit down and methodically weed out their possessions. Yet I see notices of self-storage units auctioned off because of nonpayment for the storage. Goodbye stuff and credit rating.

Your goal in living in a tiny house is not to deprive yourself of any particular thing or any of your collections. Your goal is to free yourself of things you don't want and that no longer serve or please you while you live in a house that is bigger than you need, mainly for your stuff.

Destuffing Plans

Let your destuffing plan give a new meaning to homework. Take an inventory of your luxury and serviceable items versus clutter. Where is the crossover point?

Think about the consequences of clutter in your life. If you had to move tomorrow, would you take that item with you? Would you pay to have it transported? Would you pay to store it? When was the last time you used it?

There is a rule-of-thumb policy that maintains that if you don't use something for an entire year, then you probably don't need it. Sometimes I put things in boxes and label them "let age." As time goes by my attachment diminishes. It's like putting ho-hum food in the refrigerator that is not that good, but you can't stand to throw it out either. I subconsciously put it in the refrigerator to spoil. Then it's easier to dispose of or give to the dog or my chickens; they will eat anything. Composting is another option.

I, like so many, condemn the steady stream of stuff that is filling up our landfills. I'm convinced that the only way to interrupt this stream of junk is to stop buying stuff we don't really need.

Stuff of all kinds seems to permeate our lives. We've had customers ask us to build a full basement under their tiny house just so they will have room to store stuff. Looking at the stuff they want to store, we can't imagine why they would spend $25,000 or more to have a full basement just to store things like plastic swimming pools, old furniture, old computers and printers, and boxes of old magazines and books. The value of all that stuff combined might be worth only a few hundred dollars' resale value.

There is one house in particular that belongs to a friend of mine where you can't open the bedroom doors all the way before bumping into the furniture. Bookcases line the walls, filled with all manner of books, trinkets, and doodads. All of them are dusty, and many are outdated. When furniture doesn't fit a room, it is worthwhile to consider selling the outsized furniture and either buying smaller pieces to fit the space or building in the furniture that is needed. Another friend of mine leaves a $24,000 automobile in the weather while dollar-store junk fills the garage.

Closets and Stuff in Tiny Houses

Most of the tiny houses that we have built have limited closet space. But this is subjective. What some of us think are small closets might thrill some others. Terri Bsullak, who is featured in Chapter 3, is delighted with her big walk-in closet. It actually measures only about 6 feet × 7 feet (42 square feet), which is just enough room to open the door, step in, and turn around. But to her it is huge, because it is the largest closet she has ever had. She has it well organized and it fits her needs perfectly.

In some very small rooms we've built, there hasn't even been space to open the closet door without bumping into the furniture. In that case we just leave the closet door off. Why not? If what we have in our closet is so ugly we can't bear to look at it, then maybe we should get rid of it. Or, if you must have a covering over your closet, consider using a simple curtain instead of a door. It's a lot cheaper, and a colorful curtain can do a lot to brighten a room.

We prefer kitchen pantries with open shelves. The canned and bottled goods all have colorful labels and we enjoy looking at them. It gives me a sense of security knowing there is enough food on the shelf. At quick glance, we know what food needs to be replenished on the next visit to the grocery store.

We've given the closet and storage question considerable thought over the years. I'm convinced of two things. First, many of us have way too much stuff, and secondly, most of us are reluctant to give any of it away.

Yes, there are some things that are just too good to get rid of. For example, my collection of favorite magazines is a personal example. Even though they take up four large boxes, I was able let them go only when I went through and kept the articles I wanted and recycled the rest.

The same thing applies to my classical guitar. I'm still attached to it sentimentally. Even though I no longer play it, I still have fond memories of the good times we all had sitting around campfires and singing songs. I'd like to someday start playing again and bring more live music back into my life. Over about seven years that didn't happen. I sold the guitar for $800 and used the money to pay down my mortgage.

Garages, Stuff, and Clutter Control

The same principles that apply to closets apply to garages but on a larger scale. A typical two-car garage can add from $25,000 to $45,000 or more to the cost of your house. That is probably more than the value of the used car you park there. Give careful thought to whether you really want to pay just for a place to get your car in out of the weather and have more storage space. Also consider that, when living in a tiny home, garages are a natural companion.

Sometimes it can be practical to convert garages into living space.

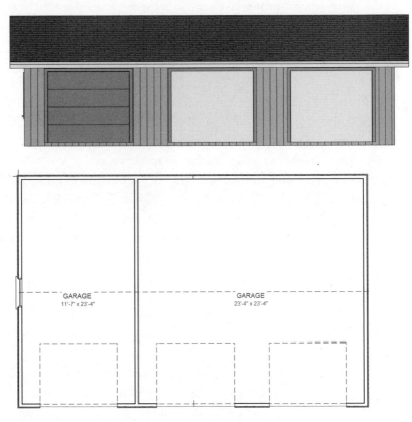

The floor plan and elevation of the three-bay garage before its conversion.

This photo shows the location of the garage in relation to the house. Note the tiny house to the right, which has a sauna and spare bedroom for visitors.

We bought a property that had a three-car garage that was initially used to store our furniture while we remodeled the house. Then we converted two bays of the garage into a classroom so we could hold classes on small-scale poultry production and greenhouse growing. Later, after we no longer needed the space as a classroom, we converted it to office space. The third bay of the garage became a small studio apartment, which now generates rental income. Before that it was used just as a place to house things that had virtually no resale value.

When you look at many garages, they are so full of junk that there's no room for the car. We know of one garage in particular that has a chest freezer in it. The problem is that the garage is so full of "treasures" that the family can't physically get to the freezer. And, there is so much on top of the freezer that it would be a major task to clear the top for access.

In the meantime, the freezer is still plugged in and merrily chugging along burning kilowatt hours at a rapid pace. The owners have forgotten what they are keeping frozen. This has been the case for years.

It might be better to not build a garage at all, especially if you are using borrowed money. Over the life of a 30-year mortgage, that $25,000 garage will wind up costing you $45,000 or more. It will not save that much in wear and tear on your car. We

Transformed for use as office space and an apartment that generates rental income, this former three-bay garage serves much more useful and profitable purposes.

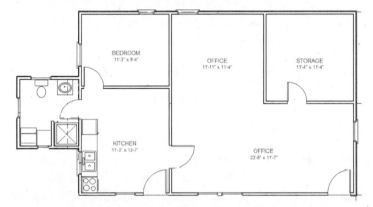

The floor plan offers a nice studio apartment and plenty of office and storage space.

would rather use the money to increase comfort or livability, or not borrow it in the first place. Even if you don't have to borrow the money, you can use your cash in many different ways to generate income or invest for your retirement.

Building a Garage Apartment to Live in Before Building Your Main House

Depending on the type of property you are building, you might be able to use the apartment for yourself while building your house, then either keep it as a guest room or office space or rent it out for extra income. Typically, in my area, a studio-size apartment will rent for about $600 per month, or $7,200 per year. You have to live somewhere, and it might make economic sense to live in your own garage/apartment and avoid paying rent somewhere else. Later you can rent the garage apartment out to earn extra money.

The garage itself can be particularly useful as a storage room and workshop while you build your house. It would give you plenty of space for storing windows and doors and building supplies on one side and room to set up a table saw, miter box and other wood working tools on the other side.

However, if it costs $15,000 to build the garage shell, and another $20,000 to complete the upstairs apartment, you would have to invest a total of $35,000. If you borrow this money from the bank, at say four percent interest over 30 years, your mortgage payment for principal and interest would be around $170 per month, or around $2,400 per year.

If you rent out the upstairs apartment at about $600 a month ($7,200 per year), that gives you a tidy extra income of around $5,000 after your mortgage payment. You can run the numbers with actual figures, but having a small rental out of what was a former garage can be profitable.

In addition, there are financial advantages from owning rental property. In the case of a garage with an apartment rental, these advantages are as follows:

1. Depreciation of the building over 20 years, used to offset taxes on ordinary income
2. Mortgage interest tax deduction
3. Rental income
4. Appreciation (increase of value) of the property, hopefully

Conversely, if you merely fill the garage and upstairs apartment with junk, and park your cars in the driveway, this property would cost you, over the life of the mortgage, two to three times what it cost you to build it .

In another scenario, imagine that you have a home-based business that uses the garage as office space or workshop/studio. Everyone might want to consider some form of home business. Maybe not full time if you already have a full-time job but certainly one that is capable of becoming full time if and when the need arises. You never know when the economy might constrict and you'll need a new income stream.

Why is a home business desirable? There are a number of reasons. Home-based businesses can offer tax write-offs, extra income, no commute, and the freedom to work as hard and as long as you want.

A 546-square-foot garage then becomes valuable as office space, at a far greater rate than can be accorded to just garage space. For example, we own a small publishing company, Good Earth Publications, that we operate out of our former two-car garage. We have plenty of room here for an office, a reception area, an order fulfillment room, and even a small warehouse with cases of books on pallets. If we were renting similar space downtown we would be paying anywhere from $500 to $1,000 per month, not including the adjacent one-bedroom apartment that rents for another $300 per month. This turns a formerly low-value garage building into a high-value office and residential building that generates between $10,000 and $15,000 annually in earned income and savings.

All of these things are topics for you to consider as you dream about and plan for your new tiny house.

Deciding What Stuff Serves You

There are three main reasons we keep stuff. Considering these might help you decide how to pare down your belongings so you can fit into a tiny house.

1. **Frequency of Use.** If you look at a possession and can't remember the last time you used it, get rid of it. If you have to put a number on it, anything you haven't used for 12 months is fair game for disposal. Or, you might think, I'll need it sometime in the future. Maybe that's true, but again, if you haven't used it for a year chances are you aren't going to use it next year either. An unused rotary tiller that sits idle in the barn is a good example. I have the philosophy that if I donate an item to Goodwill or Habitat for Humanity, I can go there later and find another one just about like it, for a fraction of the cost of buying a new one, and without having to store it.

2. **Ego.** We are often attached to our stuff because of ego. We paid a lot of money for the item, and we feel guilty or embarrassed about selling it or giving it away for less than it's really worth. Idle exercise equipment usually falls into this category. Every basement I can ever remember being in had at least one formerly high-priced item that now has only ego value.

3. **Sentimental Reasons.** The third reason we keep things is because we are sentimentally attached to them, and it would just break our heart to have to part with them. Furniture from our parents and grandparents is a good example of this category.

   About 40 years ago a friend's grandmother died, leaving him some valuable antique furniture that he just couldn't bear to part with, so he stored it in his barn loft. It's still there today, covered with a tarp with dust, hay chaff, and bird droppings, slowly deteriorating to a point of being valueless. How sad, really, that the furniture isn't sold to an antiques dealer and placed back into circulation so that someone who values the style and the type of wood can enjoy it. I know his family could use the money. As it is, my friend feels guilty about it as the fine pieces deteriorate.

Stuffology 101
Clutter and YOU — or — Stuff and Yourself

Financial Consequences of Stuff
- Bigger house & higher Mortgage = thousands of dollars over lifetime of loan
- Resale value of stuff = not much. Yard sales and auction prices.
- Money spent on stuff, not in savings or investments = big time opportunity losses.

Cleaning Clutter & Stuff
- Must move stuff to dust or clean.
- More expensive to clean.
- Takes more cleaning time because of volume.
- Bigger houses have more space for stuff = you buy stuff to fill the space.

Social Consequences of Stuff
- Messy house causes you to be embarrassed to have folks over = lonely and isolated.
- Too much trouble to entertain because cleaning takes so long. Because you don't invite folks over they don't invite you either = lonely and isolated.
- You, or your estate, must ultimately deal with the stuff.
- Sooner or later it's the land fill = the ultimate grave for all your stuff.

Unintended Consequences of Stuff

Health Consequences of Stuff
- Dirty and messy house leads to molds and dust, resulting in allergies, asthma, and challenged immune system.
- Things on floor or steps lead to accidents = higher insurance premiums.
- Clutter in cabinets leads to dangerous spills. Prescription drugs fall out of medicine cabinet. Toxic cleaners spill on floor.

Frustration of Stuff
- Can't find things when needed. Lots of time spent looking.
- Blame your spouse or housemate for losing things. Unpleasant arguments and building tension lead to separation.

Environmental Consequences of Stuff
- Natural resources used to manufacture.
- Packaging, shipping, and handling = fuel and energy consumption.
- Tipping fees at land fills = environmentally insensitive.

Moving Day for Stuff
- Harder because more stuff.
- More expensive to move, multiple trips and bigger van, more muscular men needed.
- Harder to pack.
- More boxes and packing materials

Ways to Find New Homes For Stuff — Profitably

We have made finding homes for many of our redundant items a challenge and fun. You can make this a little business venture.

DeClutter Action Plan
Real life (partial) list

Kitchen
- Sort utensils — who needs 8 wooden spoons?
- Too many pots — get rid of aluminum ones.
- Go through pantry — some items are ancient.
- Consolidate cleaners under sink.
- Wicker baskets — give away or use for Easter.
- Glass jars — recycle.

Barn and Tool Shed
- Sort and get rid of rusty tools.
- Sell 2 of the 3 lawn mowers.
- Dejunk — will take several weekends.
- Build mobile tiny tool shed to get organized.

Linens
- Give old towels to Humane Society.
- Give extra sheets and pillows to co-worker with 6 kids.
- Spotted table cloths use for rags —> wax car.

Art
- Rotate wall hangings and masks for a fresh look.
- Donate better pieces to museums or sell on eBay.
- Too many art doodads, put in gift chest to give to special people when appropriate.

Construction Materials
- Sort what lumber is good. Have folks over for bonfire to burn the rest.
- Inventory windows and doors and use on next house or sell.

Office Stuff
- Go through office supplies and see what is really used, especially packing materials.
- Donate extra desk chair and file cabinet to start-up entrepreneur.
- Find nonprofit homes or kids for old computer equipment. Take tax deduction.

Files and Papers
- Review and sort all the filing cabinets. Box or recycle all outdated documents.
- Recycle, shred, or burn tax records older than 7 years — keep real estate records.
- Special subject files — golly how my interests have changed —> recycle.

Libraries
- Review books and cull ones no longer of interest. Give to prisons, library, or Goodwill.

Mind Clutter
- Beliefs and emotions that don't support your self-esteem and evolution.
- Substances that give you murky thinking.

Time Clutter
(Doings and doodlings that waste your precious time).
- Mindless TV shows that are only mildly entertaining and leave you no better off than before watching them.
- News — bad news. Turn off the news if it makes you feel bad after hearing it.
- Procrastination in all its forms.
- Listening to someone's problems, again and again and again …

Life Clutter
or Take Clutter Clearing to the Next Level
Really want to have more time, freedom, and money?
Consider getting rid of the other clutter in your life.

Perhaps dealing with non-physical clutter is a spiritual practice?

Group or Organization Clutter
- Groups you've joined but really don't benefit from.
- Getting snookered into volunteering when you don't want to do.

People Clutter
- Avoiding those who leave you feeling drained, intimidated, controlled, frustrated, and/or angry.
- Energy harvesters/vampires: those who invoke in you all the above emotions, leaving you feeling drained — you know who they are.

Body Clutter
- Fat ☞ lose excess flab.
- Shaggy hair ☞ get hair cut.
- Dirty fingernails ☞ manicure.
- Teeth clutter ☞ schedule cleaning with dentist

Use the money you earn from selling your excess stuff to fund an investment or start a small, at-home, part-time business. The mechanics of unloading your unused items are very simple: find out what they're worth and let them go. Here are a few ways to let them go.

1. *Yard Sales*
    Yard sales are fun and can be useful if you are located in an area where there's a big enough population to attract to your sale. The last yard sale we held was very successful. We were moving and had to streamline. We sold a lot of big items such as woodworking tools we no longer needed, a canoe that needed repairs, exercise equipment, and extra building materials that Andy had picked up at a discounted price. We held our sale on a very bright Saturday in May and put up big signs at all the intersections within a four-mile radius. We had a steady stream of visitors throughout the day and took in several thousand dollars.

2. *Antiques Dealers*
    If you don't favor the idea of yard sales, then consider calling a local antiques dealer to look at your items and see if any of them have value. There is always a possibility that you will have something worth selling. How do you find a dealer who will treat you fairly? Ask around to see if any of your friends or relatives have suggestions. Most antiques dealers have a reputation in the community and will treat you fairly. If in doubt, ask for more than one opinion, and also look for your items in one of the books on antiques to see what their value might be.

3. *Online Auctions*
    Selling items on internet auctions, and especially eBay, is easier in many ways than holding a yard sale. It's simple to open an account on eBay, and there is a tutorial you can follow to help you learn the ropes. All you then need is a digital camera or a

photo scanner to load pictures of your items on to the eBay sales page. We have sold quite a few items, even tiny houses, on eBay.

4. *Special Gifts for Special People*
As you move down the list of items you want to get out of your house, you may find some things that have too much sentimental value to sell. Or they don't have enough monetary value to make selling them worthwhile. In that case, give them away to someone special who shares your sentiment or values. We give them as gifts to friends and relatives who can actually use them and want them. This can be a bit touchy. Some friends and relatives will be insulted if you offer them something that is used. Or they will take it out of politeness and simply put it in their own closet, unused and out of sight, to become part of their stuff.

5. *Nonprofit Donations*
The advantage of donating to charity and nonprofit organizations is that you can get a receipt and deduct that amount from your taxes — right off the bottom line. We especially like to donate to self-help organizations such as Habitat for Humanity, Goodwill, and the Salvation Army. They will even send their truck to pick up bulky items, such as furniture. They have resale stores staffed by volunteers, and any money earned from the resale of donated items goes to help fund the building of a house for a deserving family or to aid programs such as homeless shelters and soup kitchens. Clothing is particularly welcome for use in inner city areas and overseas to clothe people in need.

Another favorite charity is our beloved Humane Society. Andy and I donate our time, tithing, and items to their various fundraising bazaars, dinners, and Christmas sales. You see, it's not just about stray animals. The Humane Society also provides people with invaluable fur-family and trans-species loyal friends. The kind of joy, warmth, and love that money  can't buy. How many hardened and hurt hearts have been softened by the unconditional love of a pet? How many lonely hours have been filled with the companionship of a feather or fur buddy? Both the pets and their people benefit from the adoptions.

6. Recycle

As you are cleaning out boxes, files, and corners, keep in mind that many of the items might be recyclable. This includes glass jars, newspapers and magazines, old files, metal cans, or other items. It might be an extra effort for you to sort and recycle but we think it's worth it to help preserve our forests and keep recyclable materials out of the landfills.

If you have a large item, such as an old car or piece of farm equipment, you can call a scrap metal dealer. They will sometimes come and pick up the item for free and sometimes you can get a tax deduction. Some cities and counties have a junk car plan to help pick up old vehicles and keep the county looking tidier.

7. Burning and Releasing

About every year we host a potluck bonfire party. Everyone is encouraged to bring items they want to release. We have a brief ceremony focusing on letting go of the old to make way for the new. It's very therapeutic. Items some of our friends have released to the fire have included:

+ Old (sigh and relief) love letters
+ Clothes too large because of losing weight
+ Outdated tax forms
+ Documents from that law suit you'd just as soon forget about
+ Journals processing a difficult life passage or situation

You get the idea. It's great fun and a statement of your intent to make peace with the past, with your friends as your witness. Of course, you can also hold a burn and release in your own private ceremony.

8. Move

I've found that one of the most effective ways to force myself to deal with my stuff is to move. Simply the packing and unpacking of my possessions results in my culling and discarding many things, including things I didn't even remember I had.

Why don't I mind moving? Because one of the best-kept wealth-building secrets in the U.S. is the tax-free exclusion on your principal residence. Did you know that every two years you can sell your house and not pay any capital gains taxes on the profit! That's right, every two years, as many times as you want! As fast as real estate appreciates, and as much as we can add value to houses, it brings in as much as a part-time job. I'll move to a new house to get thousands of dollars tax-exempt on my old one. We've done it several times.

Another challenge is moving into a smaller abode than you have now. My mother, Marie, had lived in the same house for over 40 years. She is a collector and had lots of nice things. Her house sold much faster than she expected, and she bought a two-bedroom apartment at an upscale extended care-for-life organization. Needless to say, there were a lot of things packed into four bedrooms, a stuffed garage, and a floor-to-ceiling-shelved workshop, not to mention heirlooms and kids' stuff in the attic and a garden storage shed. Downsizing her to two bedrooms was a life experience for all of us.

9. *Dumpsters and Landfill*
Finally, if you can't sell it, gift it, donate it, burn it, or recycle it, then you can bet for sure it isn't worth keeping. In that case, the final exit is to the landfill.

Organizing Stuff

Now that you've pared down your possessions to what you feel is a reasonable level, you can decide how you are going to store them or closet them. Any of the home improvement stores carry several styles of inexpensive closet organizers that are great for bringing order to chaos. Study them carefully, keeping in mind how much closet space you have available and the items you wish to store there.

If you find that even after diligent decluttering you still need more storage space than your little house has, consider buying or building a small storage building in your backyard.

One of the best bumper stickers I have ever seen was on the back of this garbage truck in Charlotte, Vermont. It simply said, "Sooner or Later." It may as well be written across every garbage truck in the country.

In most areas of the country you can buy a little storage shed and have it delivered to your home for less than $1,000. This is certainly a better investment than to rent a similarly sized storage bin at $50 or $100 per month, year after year. When you rent one of those self-storage units you will be helping to pay the mortgage and make a profit for the guy who owns the self-storage yard, instead of improving the value of your own property.

Up until recently, we had an especially troublesome problem with organization and storage of construction tools. Between the workshop, different job sites, and our crew's tool bins, it seemed we were continually wasting valuable time looking for the right tool. It never seemed available when we needed it. Lots of tools seemingly disappeared, only to resurface sometime later in a totally unexpected place.

Enough was enough. We were totally frustrated with the disorganization. So we dealt with it by building a tiny tool shed.

To organize our tools used on various job sites throughout GreenWay Conservation Subdivision, we built a tiny, portable tool shed that is easily moved from job to job.

We move the tool shed with our Bobcat forklift. The shed is also on a skid so we can safely move it with the tractor if we need to.

Inside our tiny tool shed is space galore, with built-in shelving along each wall and on each of the front double doors. There are hooks and space for all the tools and supplies we need. One entire shelf is dedicated to screws, nails, and fasteners. A quick glance shows if we need to resupply. A loft keeps our laser level and other bulky items. This tiny tool shed is organization and convenience maximized!

This tool shed has more than paid for itself by saving valuable time on the job by minimizing searches. Tool loss has also been drastically reduced. A missing tool is easily noticed when everything has a place.

This photo shows our tiny tool shed positioned in front of a garage we built at GreenWay. Having the tools and supplies only steps away from where we are working boosts our efficiency dramatically. At the same time it lowers our frustration and the amount of time we all spend "gophering."

Chapter 8

Tiny House Furniture

FINDING MANUFACTURERS or making your own furniture with storage to fit smaller spaces is getting easier, cost effective, and more creative. The boating and travel trailer industry have paved the way for furniture design and innovations that maximize space while being multifunctional. Multipurpose furniture is important when space is at a premium. There are increasingly many ideas for multifunctional, small-space furniture and storage. Here are a few examples that might tickle your creative side. A link for further research is also included at the end of the chapter.

Beds

Beds take up a lot of room, and having them serve multipurpose duty as a sofa or lounge chair makes a lot of sense. This creative piece serves as five in one: as a coffee table, chair, lounge, bed, and finally a floor nightstand. It could be used as that extra guest bed if needed.

Above: *Five-in-One. Credit:*

Trundle Beds

A trundle bed (or truckle bed) is stored under a normal bed, and can be pulled or wheeled

Left: *Trundle bed from Massachusetts, late 1700s.* CREDIT: HOMETHINGSPAST.COM

out for use by visitors or as another bed. It is usually on wheels and can be moved away from the higher overbed.

These rolling, or trundling, beds probably first came into use in late medieval times. A small child's roll-away lived under the main bed in daytime and was a common item. Royalty and nobles often had a servant sleeping on a trundle bed.

Here are three examples of modern trundle beds. The first is under a stair landing, the second as part of a desk, and the third pulls out from a counter.

Modern trundle pull-out beds. CREDIT: GODOWNSIZE.COM

Murphy Beds

A Murphy bed has several names: wall bed, pull-down bed, and fold-down bed. This bed is hinged at one end to store vertically against the wall or inside a closet or cabinet. Permanent Murphy beds can be built into a wall. Murphy beds can offer more than just a place to sleep. The one on the left is a desk-work area during wakening and bed during slumber. It could also be morphed into just about any sort of work station.

Modern Murphy/pull-down/ wall bed doubles as a desk. CREDIT: GODOWNSIZE.COM

Bunk Beds

Bunk bed units are available with many different features and uses. This one has stairs that double as a chest of drawers. Storage is available under the bed.

Both these loft bunk beds offer multipurpose use. CREDIT: FOTER.COM

Dining and Work Tables

Expanding dining tables have been around since medieval times. But today there are options for not only expanding them but also storage. This dining table expands from four places to seat ten people. It is called a Transforming Table with Nano folding chairs. It can be folded up to fit a very small space and brought out as needed. More can be found about this on expandfurniture.com.

The Transforming table folds for small storage when not in use. CREDIT: EXPAND FURNITURE

Underfloor Bathtubs

With a home on a foundation there might be space for an under-the-floor bathtub that is accessed by a trap door. My personal concerns about this would be mold and slippage safety getting in and out of the tub.

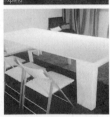

Underfloor Storage

Tiny houses can have basements and underground or below-grade space that could be cool storage for a root cellar or larder to keep food cool, including wine.

This dining table expands to seat ten people. CREDIT: EXPAND FURNITURE.

Underfloor Bathtub

Underfloor storage.

Pet Areas

There is always room for fur family. Built-in areas for them provide for their space. Especially nice is a part of a cabinet for food

Pet spaces.

and water. This can help prevent tripping over pet bowls and keep the floor cleaner.

Cats love window space. Providing them their own view can give cats much satisfaction while saving floor space for other items. I put up a simple shelf under two of my windows, and my cat naps there often.

Shelves

This above-door shelf is used at an entryway for extra shoes and things one leaves by the door. It was put up simply with a board and brackets.

I have a lot of books about many different topics. I've downsized my library as my interests changed over the years. But I still have several hundred tomes. Shelf space is important to me so I've put shelves and simple book cases just about everywhere possible without making it look cluttered.

Shelves above doors are a good use of wall space to hold extra towels and bathroom items such as toilet paper. Most interior doors built to code are at least 80 inches (6 feet 8 inches) high and can have an overhead wall space to the ceiling of a foot up to several feet depending on the door jamb, ceiling height, and crown molding. It's so simple to use this space for shelves that can hold books, boxes, towels, and even cats if they have access. Since I'm only 5'5" I keep a step stool handy to reach what's above.

This above-door shelf was attached to a support board on the wall with a box to sit on top of it, then framed in.
CREDIT: THE2SEASONS.COM

Doors for Storage Space

With downsizing becoming more popular and living space more expensive, there is incentive to find uses for every inch. How

about door space? The Murphy
door has arrived. These are doors
that contain shallow storage that
includes shelves, drawers, spice
racks, and just about anything
in between. The Murphy Door
Company manufactures a variety of amazing doors to give that
extra storage space in style. They
even have a bifold door with
shelves on both sides.

Ottoman Footstools

The definition of "Ottoman" is "a
seat or footstool without a back
or arms that typically serves also
as a box, with the seat hinged to
form a lid." It can serve as a foot-
rest when you are sitting in a chair.
It can have rollers to make it easily
movable.

*Two examples of Murphy Doors that have bifold
shelves. To the right is The Murphy Door Dresser. It
is 12 inches deep and has drawers that are 8 inches
deep.* CREDIT: THEMURPHYDOOR.COM

Coffee Tables with Storage

Small homes, and especially their
living rooms, can be clutter zones.
Coffee tables with lids offer smaller
item storage including pillows, blanket, games, books, and other stuff you
might keep in a living room.

Coffee tables with storage.

Reference Link

GoDownsize.com/tiny-house-furniture-small-space

Chapter 9

Ecology and the Tiny House Movement

W E'VE ALREADY DISCOVERED the many ways that a tiny house makes economic sense. Now let's explore how tiny houses can make good ecological sense as well. Is it possible that we can use tiny houses to help heal some of the environmental challenges we face? We feel the answer is a resounding yes!

There are many major areas of concern that weave together and form the web of all creation. Here we are primarily concerned with the ones that are unintended consequences of our nation's conventional bigger-is-better housing orientation.

Ecological Areas of Concern

1. Reduced air quality
2. Reduced water quality
3. Forest degradation
4. Wildlife habitat destruction
5. Excessive fossil fuel energy consumption
6. Soil erosion
7. Declining food quality
8. Excessive materials waste
9. Declining plant diversity
10. Declining animal diversity
11. Compromised human health and well-being

It is beyond the scope of this book to delve deeply into how each area impacts the other or how they randomly, as well as synergistically, create the environment of our lives. However, there are two questions we want to address: Could it be that our housing choices are ruining our quality of life? And is it really necessary to use so many of our precious natural resources in the housing industry?

Ramifications of Large Houses

Today's large houses have a direct impact on our planet's ecology. For starters, building millions of large homes has a direct effect on the use of natural resources.

Here's how:

* More fuel and effort are needed to gather building materials. The long-distance transport of the materials used to build these houses creates massive air-quality concerns. The smokestack and exhaust pipe effect covers most of our planet now, with increased smog, lower air quality, higher incidence of respiratory ailments, and increased costs of air pollution mitigation.
* More reliance is placed on long-distance transport for materials and supplies. More fuel is required, and more toxic emissions are released into the air, because of heavy trucks and freight trains and ships hauling building materials and supplies long distances. Here are just a few examples. Much of the spruce dimensional lumber and nearly half of the plywood and oriented strand board that is used in the United States comes from clear-cut forests in Canada, many thousands of miles removed from where the lumber is cut to where it is used.

Whenever clear-cutting is allowed, the resulting soil erosion into the creeks and rivers causes serious consequences in silting and stream bed alterations that will impact the native species and lower the water quality. This, combined with dams, whether for flood control or for hydroelectric power production, results in steadily declining fish populations and a deteriorating quality of life for all animal species, including humans. Rivers and streams run brown with topsoil as a consequence of clear-cutting forestland. We predict topsoil to be one of the most valuable commodities in the future. Without topsoil, farmers cannot grow healthy crops. The bulk of our dimensional framing lumber is imported from Canada, where clear-cutting forests is not only allowed but is encouraged by the government.

In the U.S. hundreds of thousands of acres of valuable farmland are being used each year to grow the ultimate crop: houses. How much of our farmland can we destroy and still continue to be able to feed ourselves?

Most of the ceramic tile used in America's new homes comes from Europe, brought here by ship, or from Mexico, brought to the U.S. by tractor-trailer trucks that often don't meet clean air and safety standards set for U.S. trucks. Hardwood lumber used in furniture, flooring, cabinets, and wall paneling often comes from Asia, Latin America, or South America, usually from tropical and subtropical forests that will never recover from the devastation of reckless clear-cutting.

+ Greater land disturbance as a result of the larger footprint of houses, attachments, and garages. More land area is required for larger septic systems to accommodate a greater number of bedrooms per house.

+ Higher house costs limit the number of people who can afford to buy.

+ Larger blight is created on landscape. If we continue to build 1.8 million new homes in the U.S. per year, each averaging 2,200 square feet, we will exhaust our prime forestry resources within the next 20 to 40 years. Indeed, we have already exceeded our national forest growth rate.

The ultimate crop — housing that is consuming our farm land. On the left is a working hay field. On the right are homes selling for $200,000 and up.

The average house uses an amount of lumber roughly equivalent to a five-acre clear-cut. Just in the U.S.A. we are building an average of 1.8 million new homes per year, necessitating the clear-cutting of some 6 million acres of land each year.

The forest and lumber industry will argue that they are replanting forests after clear-cuts and that natural regeneration occurs beginning immediately. This is true to some extent. But for the most part the trees they are planting (soft woods) are of a single species and are more suited to the production of pulp for newsprint than for the production of good building materials.

We are already being forced to buy a significant portion of our hardwood lumber from overseas areas. This hardwood is usually purchased from developing countries that rely heavily on the income from timber harvesting to meet their international debt and to pay the political costs of maintaining their government.

In many third world countries only a tiny portion of the earnings from timber harvesting actually goes to help support the people. Often these valuable tropical hardwoods are harvested in a destructive way, leaving behind ecosystems that will never fully recover from the devastation. In this all-out pursuit of short-term gains, the long-range ramifications are incalculable.

+ More energy is required for heating and cooling. The over-large homes that are so ubiquitous today demand a great deal of energy to assemble the materials and erect the house. But the ongoing costs for heating and cooling can reach tragic proportions. We are hearing more and more reports that heating and cooling bills are taking as much as 20 percent of the family's after-tax income. This energy for the most part comes from oil- and coal-fired electricity generating stations. The extraction and burning of coal and oil both have serious environmental consequences.

+ Larger homes have higher maintenance costs, including more labor consumed in maintenance.

+ There are fewer people per house, because higher-income families often have fewer household members.

+ More time is spent earning the money to pay for the house. In all but the richest of households a major portion of the family income is spent on housing. The higher the percentage of income spent on housing, the lower the household's remaining ability to spend for food, health care, recreation, retirement savings, and investments.

There are ways to build homes and lessen the impact on our environment. Reducing the size of the home is the first step, followed by choosing environmentally sensitive green building materials that have the least overall impact. Although many green materials are not yet standard or easy to obtain within the U.S., there are many available that are very effective for home construction and also effective for conserving our valuable resources of forests, animal diversity, air and water quality, and human health and well-being.

Can we, as a culture, embrace and utilize small and tiny homes to help give folks a quality lifestyle, while at the same time conserving energy and water, saving our forests, preserving top soils and conserving farm lands? The answer is yes!

Alternatives to Building with Wood

In many parts of the country wood is a readily renewable resource. In the Southeast and South for example, southern yellow pine is favored for dimensional lumber, being especially useful for pressure treating for use in outdoor structures such as decks and porches. In the Northeast, eastern white pine and eastern white cedar are readily available for dimensional framing, interior finish, and siding. For the most part, these trees will reseed themselves so that the forest continues to produce useful building material.

The problem, however, is that in many areas the timber companies are replanting huge areas with tree species that are useful for paper pulp production but not for dimensional building lumber. In a generation or so there will be shortages of lumber to build new homes, even in states that have traditionally been net lumber producers and exporters.

It is important, then, that we turn our attention to either growing proper forests or finding materials that we can successfully substitute for lumber. There are a number of building methods that lessen the need for lumber: straw bale, cob, clay, bamboo, cordwood, adobe, rammed earth, and so on. We won't go into detail on any of these methods in this book, but we do reference several excellent books on the subject in the bibliography.

At GreenWay Homes, part of our mission was to use materials that are considered green and that are, at the same time, approved for use under the International Residential Building Code. In doing so we can do as much as possible to ensure that our homes have the least possible impact on the Earth, while still making it possible for our new homeowners to obtain all the necessary permits and bank financing. In addition, the materials we use are chosen for their performance and for their recycled content.

There are hundreds, even thousands, of green alternative building materials on the market that aren't terribly more expensive than the traditional and conventional materials that they replace. Finding out which ones are really green, (as opposed to those that are simply "greenwashed") is a difficult task. The easiest way to find out if something is sensible is to subscribe to Environmental Building News (www.BuildingGreen.com). One of the publications they have is the GreenSpec Binder, which lists nearly two thousand products that meet green criteria.

Rather than try to cover the enormous range of green building products available, let's focus on just a few to give you an idea of the potential within the green movement.

The hardwood products one usually finds in a new home are furniture (both frames and finish material), flooring, and cabinets. A high percentage of the hardwood utilized, especially the clear, knot-free grades, requires trees that are a hundred or more years old. The material that we find most promising to replace hardwood is bamboo.

Bamboo

Like trees, bamboo is considered an agroforestry product. It is an extremely high-yield renewable resource. Bamboo has countless uses: food, animal fodder, garden stakes, fishing rods, construction materials such as wall paneling and flooring, paper pulp, fuel briquettes, furniture, and musical instruments, just to name a few. Long lengths of bamboo can be inserted to reinforce poured concrete, and hollowed bamboo stems can be used for gutters to move water from your roof to your storage system.

In many of the homes we build, both tiny homes and our allergen-free GreenWay Homes, we use bamboo flooring rather than hardwood. Bamboo flooring is harder than cherry or rock maple and more dimensionally stable than red oak for long-lasting wear. Bamboo products are available in natural beige or amber colors. These natural light tones give a warm ambiance to the room which is one reason we prefer the natural blond color which highlights the node intersections of the bamboo. The pale cream-yellow color blends well with earth-toned wall paints and colorful fabrics, making interior decorating easy and delightful.

In some areas bamboo flooring is less expensive than hardwoods, and it is readily available at a growing number of

The natural, light color of prefinished bamboo. It is also available in a darker finish.

This is a end photo of a piece of bamboo stair tread. You can see the fibers of the bamboo strips that make it a strong and beautiful flooring material.

distributors. We buy our bamboo flooring from Lumber Liquidators (www.lumberliquidators.com).

Bamboo products are made from strips. Bamboo is hollow in the middle with walls that can be more than an inch thick. The strips are boiled in a natural nontoxic insect repellent. The strips are then kiln dried and laminated to create a solid piece of flooring that is prefinished and measures ⅝ of an inch thick, 3 inches wide and 36 inches long.

Bamboo is a member of the grass family. There are over 3,600 species of bamboo grown worldwide. Bamboo grows in many climates: in the tropics, at sea level, and on snow-capped peaks. It is native to almost all continents.

Bamboo is one of our planet's fastest growing plants. Some of these immense tropical bamboos grow as

As a building material, as edible shoots, as fiber or livestock feed, bamboo will be playing a larger role in this country in the next millennium.

— Forecast of Business Magazine

much as two feet in a day! Timber bamboos can reach heights of 164 feet with a base of 12 inches, and do that in less than 10 years.

Unlike trees, bamboo does not have to be replanted after harvest. Like other grasses, mature bamboo groves have extensive root systems that continue to send up shoots for decades.

Once a grove is established, bamboo can be harvested in as little as 4 years rather than the 30–60 years necessary to grow a softwood tree like pine and the 60–120 years for a hardwood tree. Harvesting is often done by hand, which minimizes the impact on the local environment. Bamboo farmers understand the growth patterns and have an incentive to maximize timber production while maintaining healthy forests.

Bamboo is a good crop to grow on small acreage. Three to ten acres can yield much bamboo. Because of this, bamboo farmers are establishing groves all across the U.S. and Canada.

Bamboo can also be utilized as animal fodder, with a protein content of 18% to 28% depending on the species and time of year. In many cultures, bamboo is routinely harvested as fodder for livestock, especially in winter and during drought years.

Bamboo is so versatile and so viable a replacement for many hardwood and paper products that I wonder why trees should be cut at all, much less clear-cut. How much healthier would our air be if trees were viewed as oxygen generators and left alone while we used bamboo, a species of grass, for much of our construction and paper needs.

Two of the premier bamboo growers and enthusiasts in the U.S. are Gib and Diane Cooper of Tradewinds Bamboo Nursery. They sell about 200 species of bamboo commercially. What Gib finds fascinating about bamboo is that there are so many niches from which a producer can make money. This one crop can have a thousand uses. There are a variety of species from which to make many different marketable products.

Gib is very active in the American Bamboo Society. During a trip to China, he observed that when the Chinese discussed agroforestry they referred to about 50 percent trees and 50 percent bamboo. As of yet, when people speak of forestry in the U.S., bamboo has no part in the discussion.

Gib feels that there isn't any reason why Americans can't grow enough bamboo to fill our domestic markets. It takes about ten years to establish a bamboo grove. After harvesting there isn't any need to "reforest" because the bamboo grove keeps producing continually.

Autoclaved Aerated Concrete Blocks (AAC)

Another building material we have used in GreenWay Subdivision is autoclaved aerated concrete blocks (AAC blocks) for exterior walls. AAC blocks can be an excellent green building material. They provide a solid substrate for exterior stucco

Properly manufactured AAC block has thousands of tiny air holes, which give it insulating and structural value. Although the block is porous, the surface is smooth. The blocks stack easily and are versatile to work with.

or siding and interior plaster or sheetrock. They act as a heat reservoir and thermal lag flywheel to help redistribute positive gains of passive solar heating and cooling. We do not recommend using the AAC blocks below grade or for foundations.

These blocks are made with crushed sand, which is in endless supply in the U.S. Experiments are underway to determine if fly ash can be used in the manufacturing of AAC blocks. Fly ash is a by-product of burning coal for electricity generation. Each year thousands of tons of fly ash are disposed of in landfills and waste-dump areas because there is no use for it. Using it to build safe, solid, fireproof and vermin-proof housing is an excellent way to replace a significant portion of the raw wood that would otherwise be used to construct homes. Challenges to overcome are the tendency of fly ash blocks to absorb water and swell, thus becoming unstable. In some instances where fly ash has been used there have been catastrophic building failures.

AAC blocks have been in use in the United States for over ten years and account for nearly two percent of new construction in homes and commercial structures. There are factories to produce AAC blocks in Florida, Texas, Northern Mexico, and Arizona. New factories are under consideration in New Jersey, Indiana, and Illinois. AAC blocks have been used for over 50 years in Europe, where they account for nearly 50% of new construction, and in Asia, where they account for nearly 30% of new construction.

The blocks are easy to manufacture and easy to work with. When you factor in their insulating value, the blocks may be less costly to install than other wall systems. You can directly apply a wide range of siding and finish choices.

In the Southern U.S. most AAC houses are finished on the outside with hard stucco and on the inside with gypsum plaster or lime plaster. Earth plasters can also be used for interior or exterior finish. (The new synthetic stucco systems, called EIFS, which have earned a bad reputation for leaking, mold, and mildew, are not appropriate for AAC houses, or any house for that matter).

To purchase AAC blocks, we recommend that you not go through a broker but deal directly with the block manufacturer. Do not be tempted to save a few dollars on "Value Lot" blocks that contain fly ash. We have experienced catastrophic wall failures using these cheap products. In one case an entire house had to be torn down because fly ash AAC failed.

Fiber Cement Siding

In those cases where customers do not prefer a hard stucco exterior finish, we use a fiber cement siding product that is made from Portland cement, recycled paper, and crushed sand. It looks and feels remarkably like real wood siding. It has a 50-year warranty, is relatively inexpensive, and fairly easy to install. It comes preprimed and holds paint very well, often for twice as long as typical wood siding. It has a clapboard-like appearance.

Engineered Siding

In some cases where a different siding pattern is needed, for example Dutch Lap or Sturbridge Lap, we use an engineered siding product from Georgia Pacific that is made from sawdust and glue, with an acrylic primer bonded to the substrate. Because of the manufacturing process the siding is very stable and will hold paint for up to twice as long as ordinary wood siding.

Roofing Choices

Roofing choices include 40-year asphalt shingles and galvanized aluminum metal. We prefer to use galvanized aluminum for rainwater harvesting and fire protection. It comes with a baked-on color finish and has a useful life of more than 50 years.

Floor Joists and Roof Trusses

Floor truss joists and roof trusses are engineered to be built with small pieces of wood rather than requiring old-growth timber. Engineered floor and roof trusses are less expensive, are faster to install, and develop a sturdier structure than equivalent dimensional lumber. They are made from smaller boards that are harvested from fast-growing species such as southern yellow pine, which covers most of the southern U.S. In our location in central Virginia, the use of native southern yellow pine trusses reduces our reliance on spruce and pine dimensional lumber that would have to be imported from as far away as the Pacific Northwest or central and northern Canada.

Exterior Sheathing and Oriented Strand Board

In those walls requiring exterior sheathing we use Oriented Strand Board (OSB) instead of plywood. OSB is made from chips of immature trees of any species, whereas plywood requires mature trees of a particular species. When immature trees of an inferior fast-growing species are harvested for OSB this leaves more room for valuable timber-quality trees to mature in the woodlot. We are careful to limit the use and the application of OSB to outside walls, however, because the glue used in its manufacture is somewhat toxic.

Insulation

In exterior walls we install wet-blown polyurethane, a closed-cell foam insulation that has superior performance characteristics and is not detrimental to the environment or to indoor air quality. By replacing fiberglass insulation we achieve a far superior air infiltration barrier and eliminate the hazardous fibers that float in the air from the fiberglass. By using the blown-in-place polyurethane insulation we can achieve a greater insulation value that enables us to reduce the size of the HVAC system by as much as 30 percent, which saves a great deal on the installation cost and on long-term operating costs. The properly sized equipment operates at near peak efficiency, thus further enhancing comfort and savings.

Air Filtration

We install a whole-house air filtration system that utilizes the same duct work as the HVAC system. The air filter can upgrade indoor air quality to 99.9 percent pure air, which has a very positive impact for people who suffer from any form of respiratory disease or allergy. The air freshener also reduces excess moisture from cooking and bathing, thus eliminating mold and mildew potential. Any pet dander or dust in the air is removed by the filtering system, which keeps not only the air clean but the ducts clean as well, thus eliminating breeding sites for dust mites, mold, and mildew.

Paints

All exterior and interior paints are water based with low volatile organic chemicals, thus reducing off-gassing to help insure interior air quality.

Exterior Decking and Trex

Exterior decks and porch floors are Trex, an engineered product using recycled plastic grocery bags and milk bottles. It looks and feels like wood, weathers to an attractive silver-gray, and lasts many years. The outstanding values of Trex are that it will not splinter and it offers excellent traction even when it is wet. Because it is resistant to insects, sunlight, and moisture, it is a fitting material for poolside areas. It will not rot or deteriorate with exposure to harsh weather. Trex is a low-maintenance material requiring no stains or sealants for protection. It also offers variety in texture and color, and is available in smooth or wood grain textures and in five color options. In addition, it is a fine building material for ecologically sensitive and hypoallergenic construction as it contains no toxic chemicals or preservatives.

There are many ecologically sensible materials that are perfectly suited for building. Many of the products will produce a structure more enduring than if constructed from wood. Green building materials can help reduce harm to our planet and at the same time provide us with long-lasting, comfortable, low-maintenance, and attractive homes.

Chapter 10

Rainwater Harvesting
From Your Tiny Home

WATER IS ONE OF THE WORLD'S MOST VALUABLE RE-
SOURCES and it is becoming even more precious as more and more of it becomes polluted and unusable and global weather patterns shift. Already, bottled water at about $1.50 a quart is two times more expensive than gasoline. People who once took water for granted are rethinking their supply and its sources. In many parts of the country reservoirs that were once consistently full are now at record-level lows, if not dry; other places are flooding.

In some parts of the United States drought conditions are chronic. Wells are no longer being replenished from natural underground storage aquifers. In all too many cases these aquifers are becoming polluted as more and more human-made chemicals and/or saltwater seeps further and further into the earth. The human population is growing to record numbers, bringing dramatically increased water demands along with the increase in pollution.

Water is critical to our health and quality of life. Every home needs water, no matter what its size or location. So what about that old-fashioned idea of rainwater harvesting? Years ago almost everyone did rainwater harvesting in some form or another. The old rain barrel was a common sight. This is free water, costing nothing to harvest and very little to store once the initial cost of the cistern and pump is paid. An added benefit is

Everyone should be rainwater harvesting, if only for their gardens. This is a real "no brainer." — David Harbor, Head of the Geology Department, Washington and Lee University.

that rainwater is distilled, perfectly "soft" water. There is no need for a water softener or water-softener units.

Rainwater doesn't contain the minerals found in groundwater; nor does it contain the chemicals, including chlorine or fluoride, added to most municipal treated water. Rainwater is ideal for watering the garden, washing the car, and doing laundry, and it is potable once it is properly filtered.

As the Texas Natural Resource Conservation Commission put it, "Rainwater is soft. It can significantly lower the quantity of detergents and soaps needed for cleaning. Soap scum and hardness deposits do not occur. There is no need for a water softener as there often is with well water. Water heaters and pipes are free of the deposits caused by hard water and should last longer."

Another advantage of rainwater harvesting is that when people take medicine some gets absorbed by the body, but the leftovers end up getting flushed down the toilet and into the public water supply. Some of the water is cleansed again at drinking water treatment plants and piped to consumers. But most treatments for drinking water do not remove all drug residue. Additionally, treatment facilities aren't required to test for pharmaceuticals or filter them out.[1]

"Bacterial contamination, which is a big problem in well water, is almost nil in rainwater," says David Harbor, Professor of Geology at Washington and Lee University in Lexington, Virginia. Professor Harbor studies and teaches hydrology and geology as integrated systems. He also states that rainwater can have some contaminants, but these can be filtered out with the same filters used for tap water.

A rainwater collection system can be as simple and cheap as a recycled metal or plastic drum placed under a downspout. Garden

Screen keeps leaves and mosquitoes out.

Faucet to gravity drain water.

This rain barrel, courtesy of Charlotte Storm Water Services, shows universal features, including a downspout, spigot, and debris screen.

stores sell 55- to 75-gallon plastic and fiberglass rain barrels for $50 to $250. The more elaborate barrels come with leaf screens, spouts, and tubes to connect multiple barrels together in series.

To prevent mosquitoes from breeding in the water, make sure the barrels are covered or have a fine-mesh screened top to keep the mosquitoes out.

Oil floats on the surface of the water. When mosquitoes land, they suffocate in the oil. Use about a quarter cup of oil per week. You can use any type of oil, including olive oil. Horticultural oil or dormant oil is also effective for preventing mosquitoes in rain barrels.[2]

A complete rainwater system including cisterns (storage tanks) and piping the water into your house is a little more complicated and expensive than a barrel under the downspout. The equipment you need includes special types of roofing, gutters, leaf screens, storage tank(s), filters, and a pump. Above- or below-grade systems are available. Above-ground storage tanks have the advantage of easy maintenance but are liable to freeze in cold weather. Underground tanks buried below the frost line will not freeze, but you will need an access hole to be able to clean the tank and service the pump periodically.

Galvanized aluminum metal roofing is the best roof covering for collecting potable water because the surface is smooth and nontoxic. Asphalt, chemically treated wood shingles, and some painted metal roofs can leach toxic materials. Be sure to have the water tested before drinking.

It is beyond the scope of this book to go into detail about the many systems of rainwater harvesting. The internet contains a huge range of available information. Organizations you can contact include Water Wiser and the American Water Works Association at awwa.org.

Water Needs and Harvesting Ability

Even with a tiny house, you can collect rainwater — more than you might think. Even if you rely on an existing connection to the municipal system or an existing well, you can still benefit by harvesting water and storing it for use in your garden and fishponds.

Rainfall lands on our rooftops anyway, and we have to have some form of guttering system to channel the rainfall away from our houses or we run the risk of water damage to our buildings. Adding a cistern or small reservoir to store the channeled rainfall is a simple and inexpensive way to harvest water that would otherwise run off our property with little benefit.

As Terri Bsullak from Chapter Three stated about her rainwater harvesting system, "It's so simple; the rain falls and I have water. What could be easier?"

Seasonality of rainfall is a concern in some cases. For example, in the northwestern United States, rain falls mostly from late fall through spring, with very dry summers. If you are in one of those regions it may not be possible to harvest enough water in the winter to last you all summer.

The only way you will know is to determine how much water you actually need and then see if you can harvest and store that much during the rainy season.

Our own storage needs are pretty simple. During most years our area of central Virginia can rely on fairly adequate rainfall during most months. Any storage capacity would only have to be sized for two to three months' supply at the most.

Our State Board of Health calculates a typical household will use water at the rate of 150 gallons per day per bedroom. Assuming there are two people sharing a bedroom, then it seems the Board of Health is estimating that each person will use 75 gallons of water per day. That is for all uses, including drinking, bathing, washing dishes, and clothes, household cleaning, and flushing toilets.

With proper attention, water needs can be far more miserly. During Andy's experimental living in the travel trailer, he kept accurate records of his water consumption. He found that he could get by quite nicely on about five gallons of water per day in the winter, and ten gallons per day in the summer. The difference is in the winter he took shorter showers and washed fewer clothes, whereas in the summer he took more frequent showers and changed clothes more often.

If Andy can get by easily on 300 gallons of water per month, then a 900-gallon tank, costing about $500, will be more than adequate to see him through a three-month dry spell here in central Virginia. Two people would need to double that storage capacity.

In the dry southwestern United States areas though, summer rains are infrequent, so it's not unusual for water harvesters in those regions to count their storage capacity in thousands of gallons instead of hundreds. I recently read of one farm having a storage capacity of 30,000 gallons. Their needs were for livestock watering and irrigation of market garden crops as well as domestic use.

How Much Water Can You Harvest From Your Roof?

Calculating the amount of rainfall that would be available for you to harvest is simple. First, determine the roof area within your site that is available for water harvesting. Measure this roof area on the flat, not the slope. For example, Terri Bsullak's 600-square-foot house is 20 feet × 30 feet with a 16-inch overhang at the eaves and gables. Measured on the flat, her footprint is 22 feet 8 inches × 32 feet 8 inches, for a total square footage of 740. Multiply that area x 0.627 gallons, which is the amount of water that falls on one square foot of roof during a one-inch rainstorm (740 gallons × 0.627 gallons/sq.ft./1-inch rain = 464 gallons harvested).

Next multiply the result times the average number of inches of rain per month or per year and you will be able to see what your potential water harvesting capabilities are.

For example, in central Virginia we get an average of 3.75 inches per month, so Terri's roof can harvest an average of 1,740 gallons per month. A tank to store 1,700 gallons costs about $1,000.

Based on the Board of Health Guidelines (75 gallons/day × average 30 days/month) Terri should be consuming about 2,250 gallons per month. To store that amount, she would need a slightly larger tank or more than one tank. In reality, she gets

Pat standing by a cistern designed to be buried underground. The ribs support the weight of the dirt and keep it from collapsing. This 1,700 gallon cistern has two access covers on top. It is about 6 feet high, 6 feet wide, and 15 feet long.

by just fine with a 1,250 gallon tank because she can get by very easily on as little as 25 gallons average per day, or 750 gallons per month.

A typical household using all available water conserving techniques can easily get by with 50 gallons of water per day, so a 1,500-gallon storage tank is more than adequate for a one-month supply. However, if you are in an area where two or three months can go by without an appreciable rain storm, then you'll want to have two or even three 1,500-gallon tanks for storage.

You might think that all these tanks and related piping and filters will be too expensive to consider. Compared to the cost of drilling and developing a well, however, water harvesting equipment can be a bargain. In Terri's case, for example, the well driller drilled four dry holes at a cost of nearly $16,000 (fortunately the well driller didn't charge her full price), compared to her water harvesting system, which came to less than $2,000. Even a simple well can cost over $7,500 for drilling, casing, piping, pump, and pressure tank.

The water-harvesting capability of your house is something you will want to consider during the design phase. From this standpoint you will want to have as much roof surface as possible. Whereas you may have been thinking about building a two-story house to limit the size of the footprint, you may now want to consider building just a one-story home with the same square footage but a larger footprint from which to harvest water.

You will also want to cover your roof with a material that lends itself to water harvesting. Impervious surfaces such as slate, certain kinds of plastic, and metal are preferred. We discourage the use of asphalt and Fiberglass singles because they are apt to shed particles into the water that you will then have to filter out.

A roofing material having a flat surface with the least possible indentation is best because it limits the capture of windblown dust and debris. Any accumulation that does occur will quickly wash off the roof. Shingle roofs have many edges and crevices to catch debris, while metal roofs have very few. Use metal roofs with hidden fasteners such as Advantageloc, available from Union Corrugated, to limit leaks.

Almost everyone at first recoils at the idea of rainwater harvesting because of fear the water might somehow be dirty. Bacteria and particles can be washed into your water from bird droppings landing on the roof, insects, airborne particulates, and larger organic materials such as windblown seeds, leaves and twigs, acorns and nuts.

That's why an important component in any rainwater harvesting is the roof washer. The first 50 gallons or so of rainwater flushes the particulates off the roof, and that first 50 gallons is then diverted to a self-flushing holding tank before clean water is allowed to enter your storage tank. Before water is removed from the cistern for household use, it passes through a set of filters that are designed to filter out the larger particles first. Bacteria is then removed in a second filter.

Even the place you shelter your storage tank can provide a roof surface that adds to your water harvesting capacity. In the case of the Eco Garden House that we are now designing, the freshwater storage tank will be housed in a utility room on the back of the cottage. The utility room will have the water heater, water tank, filtering system, and battery and electrical equipment for the solar electric system. The room will measure 12 feet × 12 feet, with a two-foot solar overhang on the roof edge. This roof adds 16 feet × 14 feet = 224 square feet to the water-harvesting ability and can capture nearly 150 gallons of water per one inch of rain.

One note of importance is that some lending institutions will be reluctant to place a mortgage loan on a house or property that relies on anything other than a municipal water system or approved well. However, we have several friends who own properties with alternative water systems, and they do have mortgages.

Locating Your Storage Tanks

Place harvest tanks downstream of your collection system rather than trying to pump water upstream in a heavy storm. Here in central Virginia, for example, it is not unusual to get four or five inches of rain per storm, sometimes that much in just a few hours. It would be difficult to size a pump large enough to move that much water uphill to a storage tank in such a short amount of time. Place your primary storage tank downhill, and add a gravity-fed discharge pipe large enough to handle the overflow volume once your storage tank is full.

This discharge pipe can feed into a secondary surge tank below the first holding tank. That surge area can be a pond or rain garden or simple swale in your yard or even your garden. Do whatever you can to keep the water on your site until it seeps into the ground. Don't let it simply drain into the roadside ditch and run off without first benefiting your site to the greatest possible extent. Have your garden beds arranged so that water can move freely along the pathways and seep into the beds adjacent to the pathways. Even if the water pools temporarily in your garden pathways it will soon percolate down to the root zone, where it can be picked up and used by your plants.

Storing Harvested Water In Ponds

Another way to store rainwater harvested from your roof is in a freshwater pond in your yard. This is really no different than putting a pump and intake line into an existing lake, pond, or creek, except that in a pond that you build yourself you can more easily control the environment.

In summary, by overcoming a few challenges such as protecting lines from freezing in some areas, rainwater harvesting can be an easy and, in many cases, adequate method of acquiring water. You may or may not be able to rely on it for all household consumption. It depends on your total water consumption needs, average rainfall in your locale, and the ability of your home's roof surface to harvest water.

Chapter 11

Building Tiny House Communities and Conservation Subdivisions

IT MIGHT SEEM UNUSUAL to include a chapter on conservation subdivisions in a book about tiny homes. The two subjects actually go together under the broad topic of just-right housing and efficient land use.

At GreenWay we built not-so-big single-family homes from 1,300 square feet to 2,300 square feet. These are upscale and Craftsman-quality homes that incorporate features that include green building and allergen-free materials. We have had many inquiries from community land planners and developers asking how we approached developing GreenWay Subdivision in Buena Vista, Virginia. The answer is that we studied any books that we could find on conservation subdivisions and spent a lot of time on the land, walking, observing, listening, and thinking.

We are using the term "conservation subdivision" to indicate that the preservation of natural resources on the land is built into the development design and guaranteed by the covenants and restrictions. Wherever possible we enhanced natural areas and increased wildlife habitat to ensure an abundance of

> Rather than a fad, I think small homes are a bellwether, because living more densely is not only a responsible thing to do environmentally and economically but it also creates more of a sense of togetherness and social responsibility — and a cultural fabric that people who are tired of being isolated will find pleasing.
>
> — Marcia Gamble Hadley, Architect

This is a 1,300-square-foot hypoallergenic home in GreenWay constructed using AAC blocks. Decks are finished with Trex. The interior floors are bamboo. This home also includes a whole-house air filter to obtain 99.9 percent air purity inside.

bird and animal life on the land. This design and implementation will be valued and carried forward by residents of the community that evolves here.

Conservation subdivisions create communities that are sustainable, practical, and easily replicated. This integrates a design for basic human needs (shelter, food production, energy, social interaction, work) with the preservation and enhancement of natural ecosystems.

Development for housing is inevitable in our country, given the increasing population. But by utilizing the principles of sustainable land development inherent in the conservation subdivision approach, it is possible to cluster houses on smaller lots to achieve the same or greater density while leaving green space for recreation, food production, and wildlife.

Conservation Subdivision Design

In our GreenWay conservation subdivision design approach we used six major steps that are a modification of the methods described by Randall Arendt in his books *Growing Greener* and *Conservation Design for Subdivisions: A Practical Guide to Creating Open Space Networks*. We balanced the precepts of good conservation development with the principles of permaculture, which broadly translated means permanent culture and permanent agriculture. The permaculture design principles are from the book *Permaculture Design* by Bill Mollison, and from the permaculture community design principles outlined in a white paper entitled *Permaculture Village Design* by Max Lindegger of Crystal Waters Community. Crystal Waters is located about 100 kilometers north of Brisbane, Australia. The organic gardening and farming principles are patterned on the concepts of organic farming and gardening by Robert Rodale. The six steps of design we used are as follows:

1. Acquire a two-foot topographical map and aerial photograph.
2. Identify all potential conservation areas, including stream corridor, riparian buffer, agricultural land, steep slopes and sink holes, and road corridors.
3. Locate house sites.
4. Design street alignments and trails.
5. Designate areas for individual septic fields; these can be located either on each individual lot or on nearby common land.
6. Draw lot lines; in GreenWay we made all the lots ½ acre.

Step 1. Aerial Photograph and Two-Foot Contour Topographical Map

Our surveyor, Steve Douty of Green Mountain Surveys in Buena Vista, Virginia, recommended this first step as a way to obtain a base map from which we could make a number of decisions. The aerial photo and topological map were expensive (about $6,000) but paid for themselves many times over as the design evolved. We had the aerial photograph taken in the winter, when all the leaves were off the trees. Steve worked with the aerial photographer to place markers at the four corners of

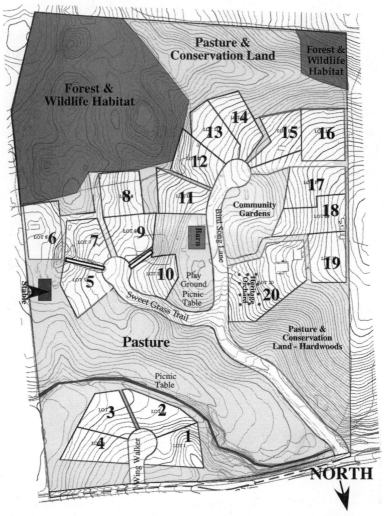

The plat of Greenway Conservation Subdivision in Buena Vista, Virginia. This subdivision was designed and developed by the authors. The 20 half-acre lots are shown in white, surrounded by 31 acres of preservation areas.

the property. Once the photograph was taken Steve entered the data into his computer program. With this new information Steve was able to determine the best routes for streets and access paths and could situate the house sites for best views and least land disturbance. The contour lines are also useful in determining the best locations for driveways, foundations, septic systems, drainage swales, and rain gardens on each lot.

Step 2. Identifying All Potential Conservation Areas

Using this topographical map, there were five potential areas that we considered. These were (a) soils and slopes, (b) wetlands and flood plains, (c) wildlife habitat and woodlands, (d) farmland, and (e) views into and out from the site. These are addressed individually below.

A. Soils and Slopes

The soils at GreenWay Conservation Subdivision are primarily loam and clay, with some exposed ledge. The land is blessed with good topsoil, regenerated from the organic farming practices of our land stewardship and that of the previous owners.

Slopes exceeding 15 percent will not be used for construction or house sites. This is because of the high potential of erosion and the desire to avoid sedimentation of the existing stream. Land that is steeply sloped remains in the common land for use by the residents as pasture for livestock, wildflower meadows, hay production, or it is allowed to return to mixed hardwood and softwood forest.

B. Wetlands and Floodplains

There are no floodplains on the property, although a narrow wetlands area exists along the brook that runs through the land and empties into Marl Brook. Currently there are riparian trees along the creek, which will be preserved. All livestock are fenced out of the stream and adjacent banks, leaving a riparian buffer zone over 100 feet wide through the center of the subdivision.

C. Significant Wildlife Habitats and Woodlands

The entire 41-acre GreenWay Subdivision is a bird sanctuary. There are already four occupied martin/swallow houses on site, along with many other bird houses and bird habitat plantings. Two wildlife areas are protected from development, with the exception of hiking and riding trails. These two areas are wooded and have extensive microclimates and rock formations. The vegetation in these two wildlife areas is left alone to encourage the natural flora and fauna indigenous to our area.

D. Farmland

We feel that large gardens and minifarms are essential for long-term community food self-sufficiency. Robert Rodale had a vision of the future that included major food production in small, intensively managed "chinks" of land between subdivisions. Not unlike the Victory Gardens of World War II but larger and organic and therefore more nutritionally productive.

GreenWay Conservation Subdivision has a remarkable leg up on farming. The site is on land formerly operated by the authors as Living Earth Organic Farm. The infrastructure is such that a community farm could quickly and easily develop on the land. Since we have maintained the farm organically, it will be possible for the community farm to be certified as organic.

For the large part, land suitable for farming and grazing remains open. This community land is owned by

To successfully have increased density in housing and at the same time leave regenerating green space, you must devote attention to an anticipatory landscape design that provides privacy, includes edible landscapes for wildlife and people, and will be functional as the trees and shrubs mature.

residents through the Homeowners Association. Significant space, about three acres, is available that can be used for community gardens and intensive vegetable and fruit production. There are many smaller chinks on the land that could be used for garden space or perennial crop plantings, such as grapes, berries, asparagus, and orchards. There is also sloped land that could be used for nursery stock, Christmas trees, and other tree or vine crops.

E. Views Into and Out of the Site

View considerations are one of the most important aspects in this development. The aesthetic value of our location in Rockbridge County, Virginia, at the edge of the beautiful Blue Ridge Mountains, is priceless to both inhabitants and visitors. GreenWay development is sited, buffered, and landscaped in

Entry views into GreenWay Conservation Subdivision are preserved. To the left of the drive is community pasture and recreational land. To the right are an orchard and nut-bearing hardwoods planted for wildlife habitat. In the rear of the photo you can see the skyline of the beautiful Blue Ridge mountains. On the ridge to the right you can see the large swing set in the community playground area.

such a way as to preserve views for all the houses and for the main entry and main common areas.

The panoramic view corridor into the property is preserved as open space. This precious pastoral view at the entrance leads the eye across meadows and rolling hills to the Jefferson National Forest, the Blue Ridge Parkway, and the skyline beyond.

F. Recreational Areas, Foot Trails, and Exercise Paths

Recreation areas are identified for use as appropriate spaces for a ball field, playground, foot trails, and walking paths. The perimeter of the subdivision includes a ten-foot corridor as common ground so that residents can walk around the entire subdivision as part of the exercise trail system. Each of the lots fronts on the common land and has ready access to the footpaths. There are nature trails through and around the forest, and a small resident goat herd is all it takes to keep the undergrowth along the forest trails mowed for enjoyable hiking.

Step 3. Locating the House Sites

Each of the clustered house lots is half an acre, and we aligned them so that none of the lots will interfere with the view corridor of adjacent lots.

Step 4. Designing the Road Alignments

The roads are laid out to follow the natural contours of the land. There are only two entrance roads into the subdivision, and none of the private driveways exit onto county roads. This eliminates a clutter of road cuts and minimizes the impact the development has on the county road system.

Step 5. Locating Septic Sites and Wells

Depending on the size and design, a septic drain field can use a fairly large amount of land. Where we can we are using new-style septic fields that can use up to 40 percent less land than conventional systems. One drain field we like in particular is called the Infiltrator, which is described on the website at InfiltratorSystems.com. The Infiltrator systems are only slightly more expensive than the traditional pipe-and-gravel-bed systems, but they use 40 percent less land, and we can plant trees and shrubs on the drain field without interfering with its performance. To some extent, drain fields dictate where lot lines and roads can be drawn. Since they depend on the soil type and the gravitational feed to the septic drain field site, the house needs to be uphill from the drain field whenever possible; otherwise we have to use a second septic tank with a pump to move the material uphill to the drain field.

We have four good wells in the development, with each well serving five houses. Each well has a large pressurized tank. A water meter at each house lets us know water usage patterns.

Step 6. Drawing Lot Lines

Once we determined the conservation and farming areas and geographical features that limit development, such as sink holes, drainage swales, streams, ledge outcroppings, and steep slopes, we began laying out the house lot lines. Smaller lots with more land open in commonly owned green space offers a variety of amenities. Individually, owners enjoy having the lower maintenance that a smaller lot offers while still having the open vistas, garden space, and walking and exercise trails that are just outside their doors on the common land.

Being a Community

Don't you want to live in a place where everybody knows your name? And in a place where those around you share the same lifestyle ideas? There is a certain comfort that comes from being known and knowing others, and this is one of the greatest assets to being a part of a community. For practically everyone there is a need to become a part of a community; a need to develop friendships and a support system that is local.

A community can provide a level of comfort and a support system that we think even the most reluctantly social person can appreciate. Whether you are a newcomer to a community or a longstanding resident, you can get a lot of support and comfort by interacting with those living near you, especially if they share many of the same lifestyle ideas as you.

For some, being part of a community means hope for gaining help in some areas of life. This could be help in child care by having other children in the community for your child to play with or help in raising your own food by community gardening, or it could be peace of mind from knowing that there will be others around you can call upon in times of need. Or it could simply mean that you have an opportunity to develop lasting friendships with those around you.

The Dark Side of Community Living: Tragedy of the Commons

There can be a dark side to living in communities. There is a real reason why Homeowners Associations have bad reputations. It only takes one person or household to be so disruptive, controlling, narcissistic, or difficult that meetings become battlegrounds. One person or a small group grips the power to make decisions, and before you know it tyranny has arrived and common resources are treated as private property, although still legally belonging to the community.

Wikipedia describes this phenomenon well: "The tragedy of the commons is a term used in social science to describe a situation in a shared-resource system where individual users acting independently according to their own self-interest behave contrary to the common good of all users by depleting or spoiling that resource through their collective action. The concept and phrase originated in an essay written in 1833 by the British economist William Forster Lloyd, who used a hypothetical example of the effects of unregulated grazing on common land."

The antidote to the tragedy of the commons is constant vigilance, recognizing when things are being done that do not serve the entire community and taking collective action to stop the problem. Easier said then done when dealing with a narcissistic tyrant.

Subdivision Design to Connect People

Subdivisions in general can provide levels of support that help connect residents, but most subdivisions do not consciously make an effort to connect residents with one another. Within planned communities, areas are set aside especially for use as community pasture, gardens, exercise areas such as walking trails, picnic and playground areas, and a planned community center for social interaction.

Subdivisions can be planned in a way that promotes development of a community. A conservation subdivision community can be a helpful and rewarding experience for all involved, including Mother Nature.

Environmental Considerations and Home Characteristics

There are ways of constructing new homes that are super energy efficient and make use of healthy and "green" building materials and technologies. Green building can use 30 percent less wood than typical conventional homes and will require up to 50 percent less energy to heat and cool.

1. Within conservation subdivisions, carefully locate street and driveway locations for least site disturbance and easiest maintenance. Wherever possible we orient the driveway and garage entry to best reduce snow and ice accumulation in the winter. All streets and driveways are gravel, which allows

surface water to penetrate into the earth to help recharge our water supply rather than causing rainwater to run offsite quickly and erode ditches and nearby waterways.

2. Choose housing designs for their passive solar characteristics and for their response to the particular lot on which they are being built.

3. Choose the floor plan, exterior design, and window sizes and locations very carefully to capitalize on views and solar orientation for each home.

4. Situate the houses so they do not interfere with privacy or view corridors of adjacent properties and so they cause the least site disturbance.

5. Use floor plans that eliminate wasted space. Many Green homes feature walk-up attics, and whenever possible we build full-size daylight basements to provide more living and storage space.

6. Design homes that include both a front porch for public presence and a back porch for private time. The porches and decks offer a smooth transition from inside to outside. They expand the livable area and make it easier for residents to move outside to enjoy the weather and visitors.

Increased Appreciation and Premium Resale Values

Both developers and home buyers recognize that conservation subdivisions traditionally bring premium lot prices and higher home resale values. This is because of the higher quality of life afforded by the natural surroundings and the community support that conservation subdivisions naturally develop. Many such communities have waiting lists to purchase homes as they become available for resale.

Chapter 12

Can Tiny Houses Help House the Unhoused and Inappropriately Housed?

W E HAVE FOCUSED ON HOW TINY HOUSES can be upscale, dignified, handcrafted, and magical. They offer many advantages for simpler lifestyles. We have already discussed how the size of your home does not necessarily reflect your wealth. For many of us our housing situation is simply a matter of choice that is determined by what suits our personal tastes.

However, millions are living in homes that do not serve them well. Many folks in the world are "inappropriately housed," as they have houses that are unsuited to their lifestyle. This might be because a house is too big, too small, too old, too broken, too expensive, too inaccessible. There are many reasons how and why a house might be inappropriate for the inhabitants.

There are other individuals and families who simply have no home at all. This might be because they have fallen on hard times or have been displaced due to natural or political instability.

Many inappropriately housed and homeless people might benefit from an alternative selection in housing. Our cultural standard has become the 2,000+-square-foot, three-bedroom, two-bath house with a two-car garage.

We have given a lot of thought and meditation to alternative housing. By alternative, we include the list of folks and their tiny house uses in Chapter 1 who want to change from the traditional American home of the *Donna Reed* and *Father Knows Best* era. Let's face it — the world portrayed in the show

Leave it to Beaver was mythical to begin with. So we ask, Can tiny homes provide a niche and alternative housing opportunity that none of the other available housing options currently offer?

It is our belief that the answer to this question is unequivocally "yes".

Inappropriately Housed

Tiny homes might provide an alternative housing choice for those who simply do not need, or want, the standard three-bedroom single-family house or a mini-mansion. Less of a house is often desired by young adults just beginning or by seniors who cannot, or do not wish to, care for more space than they need.

For example, a tiny home may be more appropriate for the well-to-do middle class widow who currently lives in a super-sized house that was appropriate for bringing up a family but now is obsolete for her current life phase. Additionally, she may no longer have enough energy, time, or know-how to maintain the property properly.

What some people really might prefer is a smaller home close to support groups of friends or family. The problem is that few such houses exist in the current marketplace. For the wealthier segment of our population, the substitute for support groups is the extended-care retirement community. This supplies institutional support and community by proxy. But this type of housing is very expensive and out of reach for many senior citizens.

Not only senior citizens might benefit from alternative housing. Tiny

> I have patients who could greatly benefit from a tiny house, a place where they could recover from illness or injury. It would allow them to have an assistant stay nearby or to have an independent living space near a caretaker.
>
> — Dr. Cathryn Harbor, MD, Rockbridge Traditional Medicine, Lexington, Virginia

homes may provide appropriate, alternative housing to a wide variety of people in a variety of situations such as we presented in Chapter 1: Is a Tiny Home Right for You?

Here is something to ponder. If it is true that "home is where your heart is" and if your heart is homeless, then there is a part of you that is searching for appropriate housing. If available, that heartfelt home would probably be close to your friends, family, and support groups.

Housing the Unhoused

Tiny homes may help to house the homeless by providing a "just-right" housing alternative to those who lack access to an affordable, simple, decent dwelling. Below we have outlined a few ways that tiny houses might provide "alternative, affordable housing" and also possible scenarios that provide housing solutions for some of our society's problems.

Family and Friends in Short-Term Need

Tiny houses placed on existing lots might provide a housing opportunity and safety net that is not available anywhere else in society, as in Gene Babish's case described in Chapter 3: Tiny Homes and the People Who Love Them. A tiny home helped re-  unite a family and had ramifications from Gene teaching his nephews guitar to his helping around the house and with the family business.

Tiny homes might provide alternative housing to folks who are perhaps just down on their luck, between jobs, in need of downsizing, or need rehabilitation while they recover from an accident or disease. Sometimes these individuals might find just the self-esteem boost needed when they have a decent place to live while they face their life's traumas and challenges.

Affordable Rentals

Many individuals in the U.S. do not have access to lower rent, and decent, affordable homes. Information provided by the National Low Income Housing Coalition and their annual report, *Out of Reach*, clearly defines the crisis state of affordable housing in America.

Its founder, Cushing Dolbeare, the esteemed grande dame and long-term champion for low-income housing, had a lot to say about housing the unhoused in the U.S. She was appointed by Congress to "identify, analyze, and develop recommendations that highlight the importance of housing, improve housing delivery systems, and provide affordable housing for the American people." Here we also rely upon information on affordable rentals from Harvard University's Joint Center for Housing Studies, where she is now a senior scholar.

> *Based on HUD's fair market rent measure, households with one full-time minimum wage earner cannot afford to rent even a one-bedroom apartment anywhere in the country.*
>
> — *The State of the Nation's Housing 2003,* Harvard University

Even with easy credit policies it has only grown more and more difficult to afford a home in the U.S. Americans are spending increasingly more of their income on housing. In many cases up to 50 percent of their income goes towards housing. As reported by the Joint Center for Housing Studies of Harvard University, "A staggering three in ten, or 14.3 million, U.S. households have housing affordability problems. One in seven are severely cost burdened and spend more than half their incomes on housing."

In the United States, just because one works full-time does not mean they can afford a home and all the costs of day-to-day living. Many folks are making daily choices between rent and food or rent and other necessities. This is dramatically documented in Barbara Ehrenreich's book *Nickeled and Dimed; On (Not) Getting By in America.*

For some in the U.S., tiny homes can provide a suitable housing situation. Tiny homes could be especially suitable for single people or for a small family.

Tiny homes can help expand the rental market and land use density in many places. Building tiny homes in cottage communities, with land preserved for open space and farmland, could leave land intact for amenities such as food production, natural spaces, wildlife habitat, recreation, and community development.

Tiny house rentals might help alleviate housing shortages while at the same time provide passive income to homeowners, which is a valuable win/win situation for all parties.

There are organizations in the U.S. that are making strides toward solving the housing crisis. The National Housing Conference, for example, describes itself as "a coalition of housing leaders from the private and public sectors that believes that every citizen, regardless of income, should have the opportunity to live in a suitable neighborhood."

But it doesn't take an organization to make a difference. Individuals can make a tremendous difference in the world, and in this case, in housing affordability. There are ways in which one individual, you, can help with solving the U.S.'s housing crisis.

Your personal participation can help. Volunteer with a program such as Habitat for Humanity. Or do something as simple as providing one rental unit at an affordable rent. You could even donate a few hours of your time to help a friend or neighbor construct a

Never doubt that a small group of thoughtful, committed citizens can change the world. Indeed, it's the only thing that ever has.

— Margaret Mead, anthropologist

Our nation's long-term growth and prosperity is undermined due to the lack of decent affordable housing.

— National Housing Conference

home as in the old house-raising days. Perhaps "tiny home-raising" will become a fashionable community service, church, and recreational event, patterned after the very successful Habitat for Humanity building program.

Providing tiny homes could be an active part of helping to meet critical housing needs. If more people (you and I) are willing to invest and become a resource to provide affordable housing, it is possible that the goal of solving America's housing problems could be met.

Production of tiny homes is currently not done by any in the modular and manufactured housing industry. We approached several manufactured and modular house builders, and none of them was interested in manufacturing tiny homes.

We have repeatedly been told, "There is no demand for tiny homes. There is not enough profit. We don't believe it's a viable enterprise." We disagree. We believe that there is a profitable market for tiny homes.

When will our conscience grow so tender that we will act to prevent human misery rather than avenge it.

— Eleanor Roosevelt

Housing the Abused, Homeless, and Indigent

Abused, homeless, and indigent people need homes. They need a safe and clean place to heal, regroup, and even, perhaps, to die. Church and service organizations might have some land where they could put one or more tiny homes to be available to folks down on their luck or in temporary need of shelter. Sometimes individuals need a safe place to sleep or to be protected, whether from an abusive spouse or temporary poverty.

I have the highest respect for Mohandas K. Gandhi. He was truly dedicated to the betterment of all humanity. Gandhi's teachings and practices on nonviolence have affected us all and will continue to influence the future for generations. Gandhi links poverty to violence by stating that "poverty is the worst form of violence."

For nearly two decades I worked with the Ministries of Health in over 30 developing countries, and I have seen first-hand the violence and suffering that is caused by homelessness. The reason for the homelessness doesn't matter. It can be from war (refugees and displaced peoples), poverty, or mental illness.

I believe that Gandhi was totally correct by stating that poverty is the worst form of violence. I feel so strongly about housing that I'll take that statement one step further by stating that homelessness is the worst form of poverty.

Poverty = violence = homelessness = violence = poverty....

The inhumane cycle of poverty, violence, and inadequate housing breeds fear and desperation. As we all know, desperate people do desperate acts. They sometimes have to just to survive.

It is our hopes and prayers that tiny homes will help fill some housing niches and provide dignity to people who need it most.

The folks who need dignity most are not necessarily the poor nor the desperate. It might be much closer to home. It might even be as close as your mother who has lost her self-esteem and reason for living because she no longer has a purpose in her life. We all need to be needed. It's no wonder depression is epidemic among the retired.

Let's put an end to homelessness and unaffordable homes. If you don't have any home at all, small is not only beautiful — it's gorgeous!

> Poverty is the worst form of violence.
> — Mohandas K. Gandhi

> Homelessness is the worst form of poverty.
> — Patricia Foreman

Frequently Asked Tiny House Questions

How does the cost of a tiny house compare to the cost of a standard-size house?
Tiny houses are much less expensive than larger houses simply because they are smaller. They use fewer building materials and have less heated and air-conditioned space. Consequently, they are less expensive to heat and maintain year after year.

However, tiny houses still need plumbing, electrical, bath and kitchen fixtures, and appliances, such as a stacked washer/dryer, the same as a larger house. So the cost per square foot is higher, but there are fewer square feet so the bottom line is less. Sara Susanka, in her book *The Not So Big House*, states, "The size of a 'Not So Big House' might be about one third smaller than your original goal but about the same price as your original budget. The magic is that although the house is smaller in square footage it actually feels much bigger."

You can save money by doing some of the work yourself. Don't forget that in addition to the house costs, there are the costs of your lot's site development, which would include clearing, roads, well, hook-ups, septic, and landscaping.

What is the realistic resale value of a tiny house?
There is precedent that architectural detail, efficient use of space, and contemporary amenities attract not only buyers but

also national media attention. There is a growing backlash to the "McMansionization" of American housing. This movement is most visibly described by architect-author Sarah Susanka as she makes the point that smaller-scale homes are more livable, enjoyable, and socially more responsible. Every inch is used and nicely finished. For example, in a modest Seattle neighborhood, houses of only 400 to 500 square feet sold right away to single men and women for over $100,000.

I don't have a lot of money; can my tiny house be added on to later?

Yes! You can design and frame your tiny house so that a future addition can easily be added. For example, you can frame a window to become a door in the future. A roofline can be designed so that it can easily be extended or attached to another roofline. Decks can be bolted in place temporarily so that they can be removed and reinstalled when rooms are added.

I need to live on a smaller budget as I will soon have a fixed income. Will a tiny house help me do this?

Yes. Smaller homes are much more efficient to heat and cool than larger homes and can save a lot of dollars on utilities. All the tiny houses built by Tiny House Company are super insulated. Most folks don't realize that much of their house simply stores stuff — in heated and cooled space. These stored items are usually things one doesn't really use in their day-to-day life and are things that don't need to be stored in living space.

I own a house in town. Can I put a tiny house on that lot and still meet the building codes?

In some cases the answer is probably that many city ordinances and regulations allow for guest cottages and granny units that can be built on an existing lot and tied into the sewer and water connections. Check with your local zoning official to see if a freestanding addition to your home is possible. In a couple of instances we have seen tiny house additions where the tiny house itself was freestanding but connected to the main house in such a way as to qualify as a single-family addition.

What about pets in a tiny house?

Pets are part of many people's lifestyles. They bring joy and smiles every day. You can easily install a pet door in your home and build "cat-walks" or other special places your pets might enjoy.

I have bad allergies. Can I build a house that can help minimize my allergic reactions?

Yes! Many folks don't realize how the materials used in new homes can aggravate allergies. Materials such as carpeting, insulation, and finishes all give off gases that are toxic. Some studies show indoor air pollution to be five or more times higher than outdoor air pollution. You can search the internet for up-to-date information and the latest building materials to build healthy, hypoallergenic tiny homes.

How do you set a tiny house?

You can put a tiny house on any type of foundation, even on piers. This allows it to be relatively easily moved. If you relocate and want to take your tiny house, you may be able to do so by hiring a moving company and a crane.

What will my neighbors think about my tiny house?

Resistance sometimes comes from neighbors who are concerned that cottage-style housing will lessen the value of their larger, single-family homes. We have found that when up-scale tiny houses are architecturally custom designed and blended into the existing neighborhoods, these tiny houses become attractive assets and increase the value of the homes and the neighborhood.

Notes

Introduction

1. *Households and Families: 2010 Census Brief.* The 2010 Census enumerated 308.7 million people in the United States, a 9.7 percent increase from 281.4 million in Census 2000. Of the total population in 2010, 300.8 million lived in 116.7 million households, for an average of 2.58 people per household. This was down from an average of 2.59 in 2000, when 273.6 million people lived in 105.5 million households. The remaining 8.0 million people in 2010 lived in group-quarters arrangements such as school dormitories, nursing homes, or military barracks. www.census.gov/prod/cen2010/briefs/2010br-14.pdf

2. Dr. Daniel Bachman, Akrur Barua, "Single-person households: Another look at the changing American family," *Behind the Numbers,* November 2015, Deloitte Insights. www2.deloitte. com/insights/us/en/economy/behind-the-numbers/single-person-households-and-changing-american-family.html

3. Ibid.

4. HomeAdvisor. www.homeadvisor.com/cost/architects-and-engineers/build-a-house/

5. Elizabeth Rhodes. "Little houses outperform their bigger brethren not by a little, but by a lot," May 20, 2001, *Seattle Times.* community.seattletimes.nwsource.com/archive/?date=200 10520&slug=homeshock200

6. Dana Barker Davies. "How Much Time Do You Spend Looking For Lost Possessions?" www.selfgrowth.com/articles/how-much-time-do-you-spend-looking-for-lost-possessions-0

Chapter 1: Is a Tiny Home Right for You?

1. United States Census Data. "America's Families and Living Arrangements: 2017." census.gov/data/tables/2017/demo/families/cps-2017.html

Chapter 10: Rainwater Harvesting from Your Tiny Home

1. Kathleen, Doheny, "Drugs in Our Drinking Water?" WebMed. webmd.com/a-to-z-guides/features/drugs-in-our-drinking-water#1
2. Read more at Gardening Know How, "Mosquito Control In Rain Barrels: How To Control Mosquitoes In A Rain Barrel." gardeningknowhow.com/plant-problems/pests/insects/mosquito-control-in-rain-barrels.htm

Tiny House Glossary and Evolving Definitions

I N H I S B O O K *A Pattern Language*, Christopher Alexander
describes recurring special patterns that are repeated
throughout nature. Alexander's book describes 253 pattern lan-
guages and how the use and form of a space defines its function.
Alexander's book is excellent, thoughtful reading.

Architect Sarah Susanka in her *Not So Big House* books has
built upon Alexander's work and expanded definitions specific to small homes. We highly recommend all her books, which
are listed in the resource guide. Sarah helps pictorially define
such items as *pods of space, away space,* and the *third dimension.*
As Sarah explains, "These are not new concepts to architecture,
but they are relatively new to home design and the value to
homeowners is in discussing design and renovation." Sarah is
a pioneer paradigm shifter in architecture, and we applaud her
work.

In this glossary we briefly describe some of these terms along
with other concepts and descriptions of new green building materials. This might help you to begin thinking about your home
space in terms specific to smaller spaces. These definitions will
help you explain to your design person what your intent is in
designing your home the way you want it.

AAC blocks. See *autoclaved aerated concrete blocks.*

Agroforestry. Land management for the simultaneous production of food crops and trees. Cultivated bamboo groves are considered agroforestry and produce many wood-like products, including flooring, cabinetry, furniture, plywood (plyboo), and other products useful in building houses.

Alternative housing. It seems that in the U.S. anything other than a three-bedroom, two-bath, two-car-garage, single-family home is considered alternative housing. Small and tiny homes are certainly considered alternative housing in the United States.

Autoclaved aerated concrete blocks (AAC). AAC blocks are made from sand or fly ash (a waste product from coal combustion). AAC blocks and panels are organic, dimensionally accurate, and durable. The cellular structure of the material provides extraordinary thermal lag and sound insulation. We do not recommend using AAC blocks constructed of fly ash in below-grade construction or for foundations.

Away space. A place where you can get away from the main activities of a household or community. Another term often used is "a place of one's own." These rooms or spaces can be an art studio, pout house, hobby hut, writer's nook, meditation center, or hide-a-way place to relax and regenerate. Many people want bigger houses because they think that will give them a place to themselves. Tiny houses can fill the niche as relatively inexpensive away spaces for that personal privacy.

Bathroom bucket. Sometimes a tiny home is too tiny to have a bathroom. A simple five-gallon bucket with or without sawdust and a toilet seat can be used instead of having to build a regular-size bathroom. In the morning take the bucket and empty the "night soil" in an appropriate place. Urine is actually sterile, so this isn't necessarily unsanitary. Bathroom buckets were widely used before indoor plumbing became common, and the "night soil" or human excrement was sometimes used for fertilizing the soil as it is high in nitrogen.

Big houses. Is bigger better? The trend is for bigger and bigger houses that have a lot of square footage. But usually these end up being "huge personal storage containers," to use Sarah Susanka's words. As a culture, we mistakenly equate value primarily with square footage. Instead we should equate value with livability, a sense of quality, and comfort.

Building code. The construction requirements for building a house.

Bungalow. Usually a one-story house with a low-pitched roof and surrounded by a wide veranda (deck) or front porch.

Cistern. A receptacle for holding water or other liquids, especially a tank for collecting and storing rainwater.

Codicil house. A smaller house close to a larger house, a co-domicile. Also called granny unit in some locations.

Conservation subdivision. Subdivision designed to preserve natural green space and include areas for wildlife habitat, food production, and recreation. House lots are often made small in order to leave more open common land that is usually owned and maintained by the homeowners association.

Cottage communities. Neighborhoods or subdivisions made up primarily of smaller houses such as cottages and bungalows.

Cowboy or summer kitchen. The summer kitchen can still be found on many farms and ranches today. Traditionally, when several farm families got together to harvest each other's crops, the big meal of the day was the "Farmer's Nooning" or noon meal, often prepared in an outdoor or field kitchen.

Downsizing. Taking an assessment of the things (stuff) in your life and deciding which items really serve you usefully versus which items are redundant or just clutter. See also *stuffology*.

Downsizing can also mean reducing the size of your living quarters or reducing the size of your debt and workload.

Eco-Village. See *conservation subdivision*.

Fear of too smallness. Sarah Susanka first articulated this fear. Especially in North America we seem to be so attached to so much stuff that we actually develop a phobia or fear of being cramped without enough storage room. Big houses ease that fear of enough space for all our stuff, but at what cost?

Footprint. The outline of a house's foundation on the earth.

Feng shui. The Chinese art of placement. *Feng* and *shui* translate to wind and water. The art of feng shui consists in trapping and pooling good life energy (ch'i), and repelling bad energy from a site. It reaches back into the traditional Taoist philosophy that actions on earth affect the heavens, and movements in the heavens act upon the surface of the earth. As above so below.

Granny flat. A small house or apartment around 500 square feet. So named so granny (grandmother) could have her own space but be close by the family. Same as codicil homes. Tiny houses can often qualify as granny units.

Happily incompatible. To willingly accept one another's differences. To be thankful for each other and your dissimilar qualities. Choosing acceptance rather than anger and resentment when faced with differences in being.

Human proportions. See *third dimension*.

Inappropriately housed. The state of living in a house that does not properly fit one's lifestyle and needs. A house may be inappropriate for an individual or family due to its size, location, financial demands, accessibility, or any number of reasons.

Lifestyle homes. Everyone has a slightly different lifestyle that includes hobbies and special things they like to do. By their design and function, homes can reflect the lifestyle of their owners.

Light on two sides of every room. This is described in Christopher Alexander's *Pattern Language*. Two walls with windows have a huge affect on tiny houses. Rooms with light from two walls and with natural light have less glare and foster better perception of details. Christopher Alexander states that two-sided light lets you read in detail the minute expressions that flash across a person's face and the motion of their hands, and thereby understand them more clearly. The light on two sides of a room allows people to understand each other. It also gives the room a more spacious and welcoming environment.

McMansions, mini-mansions, and starter castles. These terms refer to the increasing size of the average house in the U.S. — supersized homes with a lot of square footage but not much personality. The average size of the American home has grown from roughly 900 square feet with two bedrooms and one bath in the 1950s to over 2,000 square feet in the 2000s. The average millennium houses have three bedrooms, three and a half baths, eat-in kitchen, dining room, home entertainment center, and a two- or often three-car garage.

Night soil. Human excrement produced overnight and deposited in a bucket or designated place. In pioneer days it was used as a fertilizer.

Not so big house. This is a definition directly from Sarah Susanka's *Creating the Not So Big House*: "As a rule of thumb, a not so big house is approximately a third smaller than your original goal, but about the same price as your original budget. The magic is that although the house is smaller in square footage, it actually feels much bigger."

Niche housing. Houses that supply a specialized need and habitat for non-mainstream people.

Park model. These small homes are technically recreational vehicles, just like motor homes, 5th-wheel trailers, and travel trailers. However, park models are actually luxury cabins or small homes. They are on wheels and are semimobile. They are called park models because they are often found in camp grounds. TinyHomes.com has examples of park-model tiny homes, including log cabins.

Permaculture. Permaculture is derived from *perma*nent agri*culture.* Bill Mollison defined permaculture in his book of the same name as "the conscious design and maintenance of agriculturally productive ecosystems which have the diversity, stability, and resilience of natural ecosystems. It is the harmonious integration of landscape and people providing for their food, energy, shelter, and other material and non-material needs in a sustainable way. The philosophy behind permaculture is working with, rather than against nature, of looking at systems in all their functions, rather than asking only one yield of them and allowing systems to demonstrate their own evolutions." Conservation subdivisions such as GreenWay in Buena Vista, Virginia, use permaculture as one of their guiding principles.

Pod of space. "Pod of space" means a small area with its own defined space, personality, and special function. For example, in her own house, Sarah Susanka made a pod of space by placing her fireplace in the center of the house. This enclosed fireplace separates the living room from the kitchen but leaves either side for views to her kitchen and stairway.

Pout house. Pout: a fit of petulant sulkiness. A pout house is a place to go and pout, or let others pout, as such behavior is unpleasant to be around.

Rainwater harvesting. Collecting, storing, and using rainwater. Usually this is done from roofs and collected in rain barrels, cisterns, ponds, or lakes.

Spatial perception. *Spatial:* of, pertaining to, involving or having the nature of space; *perception:* an impression in the mind, insight, intuition, or knowledge gained by perceiving. This is the way you feel in one size of space compared to another. For example, a house with a cathedral ceiling creates a totally different spatial perception than a smaller room with lower ceilings. In tiny houses sensory spatial perception is more acute. Light seems brighter, sounds are clearer, and smells are more easily noticed. Subliminal sensing is more easily tuned into and made conscious. Spatial perception can be part of the magic of living in tiny homes because you can notice subtle changes in your environment easier.

Stuffology. The study of how stuff and possessions, especially personal and household things, impact and affect our daily lives.

Third dimension. The third dimension is height, and in building terms relates to heights of ceilings and how those heights relate to human proportions. Vaulted ceilings usually make us feel smaller.

Tithing. In the olden days, tithing was an agricultural term meaning to leave behind ten percent of the crop on the fields to fertilize the soils. It also meant saving ten percent of the seeds for next year's planting. The modern definition of tithing refers to giving away some amount of money, usually ten percent, to charity or humane purposes. Around the 14th century the Church defined tithing to mean donating to the clergy. The metaphysical message embedded in tithing is that by giving away money you are acknowledging a prosperity consciousness and that there is enough money to go around. We have expanded the definition of tithing to include donating time, items, and service to charitable organizations, beings in need, or to your community. Good Earth Publications practices tree tithing by planting hardwoods to replenish the trees used in printing our books.

Tiny house. We define a tiny house as being from around 600 square feet to 1,100 square feet.

Tiny, tiny house. We define tiny, tiny houses as being from around 300 square feet to 600 square feet.

Unhoused. This is a term we use to describe folks who, for whatever reason, don't have a decent house to call home. This doesn't necessarily mean just impoverished street people. For example, the unhoused could include domestically abused individuals who need a place to stay until their problems are resolved.

Universal design. The intent of universal design is to make housing usable by more people at little or no extra cost. A universal design component can be used by persons having limited abilities. The universal design concept was developed and is promoted by the Center for Universal Design at North Carolina State University, College of Design. projects.ncsu.edu/design/cud/

Visit-ability. Providing universal access to those who may wish to visit you. Offering a comfortable passage into one's home. The ability to easily accommodate all people, including those with disabilities, by enabling easy and graceful access into a building.

Voluntary simplicity. *Voluntary*: from one's free will or initiative; *simplicity*: the state or quality of being simple; absence of complexity. To live a voluntarily simple life is to be conscious of your actions, thoughts, and being and to strive for simplicity, however you might define that for yourself. This includes the philosophy of living more purposefully and minimizing distractions. For example, downsizing by decreasing the number of items you own might save you time and money, as described in the chapter on clutter. An excellent book to delve further into this is *Voluntary Simplicity: Toward a Way of Life that is Outwardly Simple, Inwardly Right,* by Duane Elgin.

Resource Guide

Charlotte Storm Water Services
charlottenc.gov/StormWater/Pages/default.aspx
Phone: 704-336-RAIN

Rain Barrel USA
PO Box 1364
Waxhaw, North Carolina 28173
Phone: 704-843-1581
Email: SaveWater@RainBarrelUSA.com
www.RainBarrelUSA.com

Tradewinds Bamboo Nursery
Gib and Diane Cooper
28446 Hunter Creek Loop
Gold Beach, Oregon 97444
Phone: 541-247-0835
www.bamboodirect.com

Tumbleweed Tiny House Company
1450 Valley Street
Colorado Springs, Colorado 80915
Phone: 877-331-8469
www.tumbleweedhouses.com

Bibliography and References

Affluenza, and its sequel, *Escape from Allfuenza*, are one-hour PBS specials that explore the epidemic of shopping, over-work, stress, and debt that is infecting Americans in record numbers.

Alexander, Christopher, *A Pattern Language: Towns, Buildings, Construction*, Oxford University Press, 1977.

Altman, Adelaide, *ElderHouse: Planning Your Best Home Ever*, Chelsea Green Publishing, 2002.

Arendt, Randall G., *Conservation Design for Subdivisions: A Practical Guide to Creating Open Space Networks*, Island Press, 1996.

Arendt, Randall G., *Growing Greener: Putting Conservation into Local Plans and Ordinances*, Island Press, 1999.

Ausubel, Kenny, *Restoring the Earth: Visionary Solutions From the Bioneers*, H. J. Kramer, Inc., 1997.

Bahamon, Alejandro, *Mini House*, Harper Collins Publishers, 2003.

Banks, Suzy, and Richard Heinichen, *Rainwater Collection For The Mechanically Challenged*, Tank Town Publishing, 1997.

Berg, Donald, J., *American Country Building Design*, Sterling Publishing, 1997.

——— Donald, J., *Carriage Barns*, Donald J. Berg, 2000.

Better Homes and Gardens, *Fireplace Decorating and Planning Ideas*, Meredith Corporation, 2000.

——— *Home Offices: Your Guide to Planning and Furnishing*, Meredith Corporation, 1997.

——— *Second Home*, Meredith Corporation, 2000.

Bix, Cynthia, and Sunset Books, *Ideas for Great Backyard Cottages*, Sunset Publishing Corp, 2002.

Boyer, Marie-France, *Cabin Fever*, Thames and Hudson, 1993.

Brinkmann, John, *American Bungalow*, John Brinkmann Design Office, 2002

Brown, Connie, *Great Garages: Sheds & Outdoor Buildings*, Home Planners, 1996.

——— *Yard and Garden Structures*, Home Planners, 2001

Building Green, *Environmental Building News*, *Green Spec Binder*, and www.BuildingGreen.com, Building Green, 2002.

Campbell, Stu, *The Home Water Supply: How to Find, Filter, Store, and Conserve It*, Storey Communications, 1983.

Carley, Rachel, *Cabin Fever: Rustic Style Comes Home*, Archetype Press, 1998.

Chiras, Daniel D., *The Solar House; Passive Heating and Cooling*, Chelsea Green, 2003.

Coleman, Eliot, *Four-Season Harvest*, Chelsea Green, 1999.

Cuito, Aurora, *New Small Homes*, Loft Publications, 2001.

De Visser, John, and Judy Ross, *Summer Cottages*, Boston Mills Press, 1991.

Denbury, Jo, *Havens and Hideaways: Cozy Cabins and Rustic Retreats*, Ryland Peters & Small, 2002.

Dickinson, Duo, *Small Houses for the Next Century*, McGraw-Hill, 1996.

Dream Homes, *Vacation Home Plans*, Home Design Alternatives, 1999.

Eck, Jeremiah, *The Distinctive Home: A Vision of Timeless Design*, Taunton Press, 2003.

Elgin, Duane, *Voluntary Simplicity: Toward a Way of Life that is Outwardly Simple, Inwardly Right*, William Morrow and Co. New York, 1993.

English, Molly Hyde, *Camps and Cottages*, Gibbs Smith, 2001.

Ehrenreich, Barbara, *Nickel and Dimed: On (Not) Getting By in America*, Metropolitan Books, 2001.

Fears, J. Wayne, *How To Build Your Dream Cabin In The Woods*, The Lyons Press, 2002.

Fine Homebuilding, *Craftsman-Style Houses*, Taunton Press, 1995.

——— *Foundations and Masonry*, Taunton Press, 1990.

Fuller, R. Buckminster, *Ideas and Integrity*, 1963, Macmillan, New York.

——— *Synergetics: Explorations in the Geometry of Thinking*, Macmillan, 1975.

——— *Synergetics 2*, Macmillan, 1975.

——— *Critical Path*, St. Martin's Press, New York, 1981.

Guild, Tricia, *Design and Detail: The Practical Guide to Styling a House*, Simon & Schuster, 1988.

Harvard University, *The State of the Nation's Housing*, 2003.

Hemenway, Toby, *Gaia's Garden*, Chelsea Green Publishing, 2001.

Heuer, Ann Rooney, *The Front Porch*, Michael Friedman Publishing Group, 1998.

Jackson, Hidur, and Karen Sevensson, *Eco Village Living: Restoring the Earth and Her People*, Green Books and Chelsea Green Publishing, 2003.

Jacobson, Max, Murray Silverstein, and Barbara Winslow, *The Good House*, Taunton Press, 1990.

Johnson, Kenneth, *Building Spec Homes Profitably: The Professional's Guide*, RS Means, 1995.

Joint Center for Housing Studies of Harvard University, *The State of the Nation's Housing*, Harvard University, 2003.

Kachadorian, James, *The Passive Solar House: Using Solar Design to Heat and Cool Your Home*, Chelsea Green, 1997.

Kahn, Lloyd, Jr., *Shelter II*, Shelter Publications, 1978.

Lane, Tom, *Solar Hot Water Systems 1977 to Today: Lessons Learned*, Energy Conservation Services, 2003.

Lee, Andy, and Patricia Foreman, *Backyard Market Gardening: The Entrepreneur's Guide to Selling What You Grow*, Good Earth Publications, 1993.

――― *Chicken Tractor: The Permaculture Guide to Happy Hens and Healthy Soils, the All New Straw Bale Edition*, Good Earth Publications, 1999.

――― *Day Range Poultry: Every Chicken Owner's Guide to Grazing Gardens and Improving Pastures*, Good Earth Publications, 2001.

Ludwig, Art, *Create an Oasis with Greywater: Choosing, Building, and Using Greywater Systems*, Oasis Design, 1994.

Margolies, John, *Home Away From Home: Motels in America*, Little, Brown, 1995.

Matson, Tim, *Earth Ponds Sourcebook, The Pond Owner's Manual and Resource Guide*, The Countryman Press, 1997.

Means, R.S., *Interior Home Improvement Costs; The Practical Pricing Guide for Home Owners and Contractors*, RS Means Company, 2002.

――― *Exterior Home Improvement Costs; The Practical Pricing Guide for Home Owners and Contractors*, RS Means, 2002.

Metz, Don, *The Compact House Book*, Storey Communications, 1988.

Moffat, Anne, *Energy-Efficient and Environmental Landscaping: Cut Your Utility Bills by up to 30 Percent and Create a Natural, Healthy Yard*, Appropriate Solutions Press, 1993.

Mollison, Bill, *Permaculture Designer's Manual: A Practical Guide for a Sustainable Future*, Island Press, 1990.

Mulfinger, Dale, and Susan Davis, *The Cabin*, Taunton Press, 2001.

Nash, George, *Do-It-Yourself House Building: The Complete Handbook*, Sterling, 1995.

Nash, Helen, *The Complete Pond Builder*, Sterling, 1996.

National Housing Conference, *Four Windows*, NHC, 2004.

National Low Income Housing Coalition, *Out of Reach 2003: America's Housing Wage Climbs*, NLIHC, 2003.

Obomsawin, Robbin, *Small Log Homes: Storybook Plans and Advice*, Gibbs Smith, 2001.

Parikh, Anoop, *Making the Most of Small Places*, Rizzoli International, 1994.

Paul, Linda Leigh, *Cottages by the Sea: The Handmade Homes of Carmel, America's First Artist Community*, Universe, 2000.

Pearson, David, *Freewheeling Homes: The House That Jack Built*, Chelsea Green, 2002.

——— *Treehouses (The House That Jack Built)*, Chelsea Green, 2001.

Princeton University, *Dictionary.com; WordNet 2.0*, Princeton University, 2003.

Ramsey, Dan, *The Complete Idiot's Guide to Solar Power for your Home*, Alpha Books, 2003.

Rawlings, Irene, and Mary Abel, *Portable Houses*, Gibbs Smith, 2004.

Rodale Do-It-Yourself Books, *Adding On: How to Design and Build a Beautiful Addition to Your Home*, Rodale, 1995.

Roy, Rob, *The Complete Book of Underground Houses*, Sterling, 1994.

Schaeffer, John, *Real Goods Solar Living Sourcebook, Eleventh Edition*, Chelsea Green, 2001.

Sears and Roebuck, *Small Houses of the Twenties*, Dover Publications, 1991.

Sexton, Richard, *The Cottage Book*, Chronicle Books, 1998.

Star, Blue Evening, *Tipis & Yurts: Authentic Designs for Circular Shelters*, Lark Books, 1995.

Stiles, David, and Jeanie Stiles, *Cabins: A Guide to Building Your Own Nature Retreat*, Firefly Books, 2001.

——— *Rustic Retreats: A Build-It-Yourself Guide*, Storey Publishing, 1998.

Still, Joanne, *What's In Style: Fireplaces*, Creative Homeowner, 2002.

Sunset Books, *Sheds & Cottages*, Sunset Publishing, 1996.

Susanka, Sarah, *Creating the Not so Big House: Insights and Ideas for the New American Homes*, Taunton Press, 2000.

——— *Not So Big Solutions for Your Home*, Taunton Press, 2002.

——— *Home by Design; Transforming Your House Into Home*, Taunton Press, 2004.

Susanka, Sarah, and Obolensky, Kira, *The Not So Big House*, Taunton Press, 1998.

Tidbury, Jane, *Little Retreats*, Clarkson Potter, 2001.

Tolpin, Jim, *Built-In Furniture*, Taunton Press, 1997.

——— *The New Cottage Home*, Taunton Press, 2000.

——— *The New Family Home*, Taunton Press, 2000.

Topham, Sean, *Move House*, Prestel Verlag, 2004.

Tredway, Catherine, *Dream Cottages*, Storey Publishing, 2001.

Van Der Ryn, Sim, and Stewart Cowan, *Ecological Design*, Island Press, 1996.

Wagner, John D., *House Framing*, Creative Homeowner, 1998.

Walker, Lester, *Tiny Tiny Houses: Or How To Get Away from it All*, Overlook Press, 1987.

——— *The Tiny Book of Tiny Houses*, Overlook Press, 1993.

Wells, Malcolm, *The Earth-Sheltered House: An Architect's Sketchbook*, Chelsea Green, 1998.

Wenz, Philip S., *Adding To A House: Planning, Design, and Construction*, Taunton Press, 1998.

Acknowledgments

SPECIAL THANKS TO MY FAMILY AND INNER CIRCLES. No one has taught me more about myself and brought so much adventure into my life than my very talented and often brilliant, tiny house builder and contributor, Andy Lee. Two very awesome people were my parents, Marie and Richard Foreman, who gave me a wholesome and loving upbringing and positive role models to follow. Thanks to my dear brother, Rick Foreman, for always being there. And other members of my extended family whom I cherish. I love and appreciate your being in my life.

Some say it takes a village to raise a child. We know it takes more than a village to create a book. The content in *Tiny Homes* is a result of many folks' dreams, inspirations, ideas, writings, and contributions through the years.

Deep appreciation to the case study contributors, Gene Babish, Terri Bsullak, Cindy and Danny Campbell, Barbara Lane, and Ray Pealer, for sharing their tiny house stories and enthusiasm for their tiny abodes.

And most of all, deepest respect and love for this very special planet, Gaia, that supports us all.

Many blessings, love and hope,

Patricia Foreman

Index

About the Author

P<small>AT</small> F<small>OREMAN</small> is a pharmacist, sustainable agricultural activist, local foods advocate, and popular speaker. She was a class A contractor in Virginia and co-owned the United States' first tiny-house construction company. Pat has been widely published in major national magazines, including *Mother Earth News*, *Backyard Poultry*, and *BackHome Magazine*, and is a popular guest on local and national radio and television talk shows. She has degrees in pharmacy and animal sciences and has her Master's of Public Affairs (MPA). Pat served as a Science Officer for the United Nations in Vienna and has worked in over 30 countries, conducting workshops and providing consulting services. She currently lives in a very small home in Richmond, Indiana.

2198231904 5344

A Note about the Publisher

NEW SOCIETY PUBLISHERS is an activist, solutions-oriented publisher focused on publishing books for a world of change. Our books offer tips, tools, and insights from leading experts in sustainable building, homesteading, climate change, environment, conscientious commerce, renewable energy, and more — positive solutions for troubled times.

We're proud to hold to the highest environmental and social standards of any publisher in North America. This is why some of our books might cost a little more. We think it's worth it!

+ We print all our books in North America, never overseas
+ All our books are printed on **100% post-consumer recycled paper**, processed chlorine free, with low-VOC vegetable-based inks (since 2002)
+ Our corporate structure is an innovative employee shareholder agreement, so we're one-third employee-owned (since 2015)
+ We're carbon-neutral (since 2006)
+ We're certified as a B Corporation (since 2016)

At New Society Publishers, we care deeply about *what* we publish — but also about *how* we do business.

Download our catalogue at https://newsociety.com/Our-Catalog, or for a printed copy please email info@newsocietypub.com or call 1-800-567-6772 ext 111.

New Society Publishers
ENVIRONMENTAL BENEFITS STATEMENT

For every 5,000 books printed, New Society saves the following resources:[1]

19	Trees
1,752	Pounds of Solid Waste
1,927	Gallons of Water
2,514	Kilowatt Hours of Electricity
3,184	Pounds of Greenhouse Gases
14	Pounds of HAPs, VOCs, and AOX Combined
5	Cubic Yards of Landfill Space

[1]Environmental benefits are calculated based on research done by the Environmental Defense Fund and other members of the Paper Task Force who study the environmental impacts of the paper industry.

MIX
Paper from
responsible sources
FSC
www.fsc.org   FSC® C016245

new society
PUBLISHERS
www.newsociety.com